NUGGETS OF
GOLD

2001 SPURGEON QUOTES

AMBASSADOR-EMERALD INTERNATIONAL
GREENVILLE, SOUTH CAROLINA • BELFAST, NORTHERN IRELAND

Nuggets of Gold

Published by
Ambassador-Emerald International
1 Chick Springs Road, Suite 203
Greenville, SC 29609 USA

and

Ambassador Productions
16 Hillview Avenue
Belfast, Northern Ireland
BT5 6JR

Cover and internal design © 1999 GRAND DESIGN
Cover design by Matt Donovan
Internal design by Brad Sherman
Some Cover photography © 1999 Photodisc
Engraved handwriting on cover from actual sermon notes written by C.H. Spurgeon.
Used by permission. Courtesy of the Bob Jones University Mack Library.

www.emeraldhouse.com

INTRODUCTION
❧

Since Spurgeon's death in 1892 a number of books of his quotations have been published. The distinctive feature of this book is the brevity of the quotations which do not exceed one sentence in length.

The quotations are arranged under 119 different topics in alphabetical order. In selecting the quotations an attempt was made to include only those which set forth pertinate biblical truths in a vivid and unique way. Spurgeon was a master of this element in preaching.

A brief statement of truth can sometimes grip the mind's attention in a way that a longer explanation can't accomplish. For this book the term "one-liner" could be defined as a one sentence quotation even though some sentences are longer than what would ordinarily be considered as one-liners.

The notations at the end of each quotation indicate its source as follows:

V = Volume (of published sermons)
M. & E. = Morning & Evening (Devotional)
T. D. = Treasury of David (commentary on the Psalms)
p. = page

ANTINOMIANISM
⚬

If any man says, "I trust in Jesus, therefore I will live as I like," that man's religion is vain; he has profaned the cross.
V. 19, p. 528

Of all judgments surely that will be the heaviest which shall come upon the man who dared to take the doctrine of the cross as a reason for careless living.
V. 19, p. 528

The Lord has not ordained any man to eternal life with the provision that he may continue in his sin.
V. 31, p. 153

The great mercy of God has been turned by some into a reason for continuing in sin; but God has never restricted his mercy [to others] because of that.
V. 35, p. 235

Those people who have a dread of God which makes them appear religious and who yet all the while live in sin, are most in danger of any people in the world.
V. 27, p. 564

Many would like to be saved from the punishment due to sin and yet be allowed to go on in sin, but there is nothing of that kind of teaching in the Scripture.
V. 41, p. 74

ATONEMENT
⚬

Ring out that note again, "Christ Jesus came into the world to save sinners;" it is worthy of angelic trumpets, it is worthy of the orator's loftiest speech and the philosopher's profoundest thought.
V. 54, p. 197

"He laid down his life for us" (I Jn. 3:16) sublimity in thought always needs simplicity of words to express itself.
V. 46, p. 1

Did he lay down his life for us? then, my brethren, how great must have been our sins that they could not have been atoned for at any other price.

V. 46, p. 2

If Christ has suffered in our stead we cannot suffer for sin.

V. 28, p. 67

God has dealt with him as though he had sinned your sin, and now he deals with you as though you had wrought his righteousness.

V. 33, p. 509

Believe me, there is no solid joy, no seraphic rapture, no hallowed peace, this side of heaven, except by living close under the shadow of the cross.

V. 61, p. 163

On whatever subjects I may be called to preach, I feel it to be a duty which I dare not neglect to be continually going back to the doctrine of the cross.

V. 45, p. 277

If on the cross he bore your sin, he will not suffer you to bear it and make void his sacrifice.

V. 36, p. 497

Strong Son of God, when you did bear our sins in your own body on the tree, this was the fulfillment of all our desires, the canceling of sin, the removal of wrath, and securing of eternal life.

V. 36, p. 501

The death of Christ rendered more honour to the Law than all the obedience of all who are under it could have rendered.

V. 28, p. 601

The death of Christ is a well-spring of joy.

V. 33, p. 377

All good things lie within the compass of the cross; its outstretched arms overshadow the whole world of thought.

V. 33, p. 376

Some reject the simplicity of the cross, and put in its place the theories of the philosophers.
V. 31, p. 436

The cross is the focus of all human history.
V. 13, p. 200

Other men, if they died for us, would but pay the debt of nature a little before its time; but Jesus needed not to die.
V. 33, p. 507

I would like to have it said of me that I maintained the glory of my Lord, and defended the doctrines of his cross, and was a friend of the old gospel while others were gadding after novelties.
V. 33, p. 275

I am bound to preach Jesus Christ and him crucified, for I do not know anything else to preach; my simplicity is my safeguard.
V. 20, p. 94

The cross will float me into the port of peace; if it does not I must be lost, for every other life–boat has gone to the bottom long ago.
V. 26, p. 417

If you have not trusted in the crucified while standing alone in contemplation at the foot of the cross, you have not believed unto life eternal.
V. 13, p. 678

O cross, whatever shame there was about you shall be wiped out forever among the sons of men, for Christ shall sit upon the throne of judgment.
V. 25, p. 305

The Godhead, being linked with the manhood, gives supreme virtue to all that manhood suffered.
V. 40, p. 30

The shameful death of the cross had greater power over Joseph of Arimathea than all the beauty of Christ's life.
V. 30, p. 378

If the spectacle of dying love does not quicken us into coura-
geous affection for him, what can.
V. 30, p. 380

No man who is the friend of the cross of Christ will give
license to his passions or give allegiance to his appetites.
V. 44, p. 40

He drank to the last dregs the cup of wrath that was your
due, so there is not one drop left for you to drink.
V. 56, p.417

ATTRIBUTES OF GOD

My thoughts are so well known to him that, even before I
think them, he knows what they will be.
V. 53, p. 178

How idle it is to dream of our ever running parallel in understanding with the infinite God; his knowledge is too wonderful for us, it is so high we cannot attain to it.
V. 34, p. 54

I cannot expect to understand the mysteries of God; if I
understand God, he could not be the true God.
V. 34, p. 54

God knows all about you and his knowledge is more impor-
tant than the opinions of dying men.
V. 35, p. 427

Eternity did not bring him forth from its mighty bosom but he
brought forth eternity.
V. 12, p. 677

All worlds are but sparks from the anvil of his omnipotence;
space, time, eternity, all these are as nothing before him.
V. 27, p. 293

They tell us that the powers of evil will grow stronger and
stronger; suppose they do; the Almighty will never grow weak.
V. 51, p. 393

Some ascribe omnipotence to the will of man and lift man up to a sort of rivalship with God, but when the Holy Spirit comes to effectual work and puts forth his mighty power who shall stay his hand?
V. 11, p. 641

Without God the whole universe would be a valley full of dry bones, a horrible charnel house.
Vol. I, Autobiography

Huge as this universe is, God has complete power over it, as you have with the ball which you toss in your hand.
V. 25, p. 188

BACKSLIDING

If there is no care about making the heart go right, it must go wrong, because the natural tendency of our mind is toward evil.
V. 47, p. 500

He who does not devote his whole soul to fighting the battle of life will certainly lose it.
V. 47, p. 501

A life may begin well and yet may be clouded ere its close; the verdure of earnestness may fade into the withered and yellow leaf of backsliding.
V. 20, p. 26

The greatest faith of yesterday will not give us confidence for today, unless the fresh springs which are in God shall overflow again.
V. 20, p. 26

You may, in order to help yourself, do in five minutes what you cannot undo in fifty years; and you may bring upon yourself a lifelong series of trials by one single unbelieving action.
V. 20, p. 30

If by doing one wrong transaction you could rid yourself from all liabilities in business and be henceforth in adequate circumstances, that would not, before God, take off the edge of the evil.
V. 20, p. 31

We have something better to do than to flit among the flowers like butterflies, with nothing particular to care about, and no eternal future within the range of our thoughts or hopes.
V. 20, p. 350

Like the moon, we borrow our light; bright as we are when grace shines on us, we are darkness itself when the Sun of Righteousness withdraws Himself.
M & E p. 363

Whenever a man gets away from communion with Christ, he begins to ask a host of questions.
V. 35, p. 118

Tell me that you love the world and I will tell you that the love of the world is enmity to God.
V. 27, p. 573

We have Protestants nowadays who never protest against anything, and Nonconformists who conform to everything which is in fashion.
V. 35, p. 603

The renewed man feels that the general lukewarmness of the church cannot be an excuse for his own indifference.
V. 13, p. 638

If we let passion take the place of judgment and self–will instead of scriptural authority, we shall fight the Lord's battles with the devil's weapons.
V. 10, p. 5

It is from the egg of carnal security that the canker-worm of backsliding is hatched.
V. 25, p. 283

Many a worldly man has a better temper than a genuine Christian.
V. 14, p. 425

You are doing your soul serious mischief if you put the whole of your strength into that part of you life which is visible to men.
V. 16, p. 234

Do not, I pray you, neglect the spiritual for the sake of the external or you will be throwing away gold for iron.
V. 16, p. 235

The prodigal son confessed that he was not worthy to be called a son, yet he knew he was a son, so back he came and his father received him.
V. 16, p. 154

I have noticed that, whenever any who have been excommunicated from this church, have been restored, in every case they have walked in lowliness, and won all our hearts by their contrition and little esteem of themselves.
V. 16, p. 156

Backsliding begins in forsaking prayer, and recovery will begin in renewing supplication.
V. 16, p. 156

Be half a Christian and you shall have enough religion to make you miserable.
V. 31, p. 443

Every man in the church is either a help or a hindrance.
V. 31, p. 443

I constantly see persons trying, not how near they can live to God, but how far they can live from God, and yet be called Christians.
V. 43, p. 429

Though the enemy may seem to conquer the territory of your manhood, he cannot establish a kingdom there.
V. 15, p. 692

Never, O Christian, turn aside from the highway of rectitude, because it threatens you with shame or loss; the first loss will be vastly less than the after-losses you will incur by seeking to avoid it.
V. 18, p. 56

If you are willing to lose Christ's company, he is never intrusive, he will go away from you, and leave you until you know his value and begin to pine for him.
V. 18, p. 90

If our walk among men is not such, "as becoming to the gospel," what hard thoughts those around us may have of our Saviour.
V. 38, p. 94

It is evident to each one of you that all the vile insults of infidels could never dishonor Christ as the inconsistencies of his own disciples do.
V. 41, p. 313

It is not at all an uncommon thing for us to dishonor Christ under the notion that we are showing our zeal for the king.
V. 41, p. 314

BLOOD

To be washed in the precious blood, is as needful for the very best of fallen humanity, as for the very worst.
V. 44, p. 489

The precious blood is our great security from backsliding, for by it we obtain daily access to God.
V. 26, p. 635

I am sure if people knew the power of the blood of Christ they could never become slaves to the superstitions of men.
V. 51, p. 77–78

CHURCH

The worst evils which have ever come upon the world have been brought upon her by an unholy church.
M. & E., p. 357

A church with God's presence in it is holy, happy, united, earnest, laborious, successful; fair as the moon before the Lord, and clear as the sun before the eyes of men, she is terrible as an army with banners to her enemies.
V. 10, p. 604

We do not want fresh ministers, or fresh plans, or fresh ways, though many might be invented to make the church better; we only want life and fire in those we have.
V. 44, p. 675

If anybody had seen Christ in his little church on earth, he would have said, 'there is not a respectable person among them'; as if it were respectable to have money.
V. 34, p. 57 & 58

Some have said, 'I do not think I shall go up to the house of God today, I feel so unhappy and cast down': when should you go so much as then in order that you may find comfort.
V. 23, p. 281

I fear that many of our friends across the Atlantic have fallen into most serious mistakes, for when certain of their great preachers are absent, their places of worship are closed.
V. 55, p. 558

I do not believe the world would be half so lenient to the church; now–a–days, if it were not that the church has grown complacent to the world.
V. 11, p. 128

Whenever God sends prosperity to the church and any of the members begin to ascribe the success to themselves, the blessing is almost sure to go.
V. 51, p. 80

The church's best harvests have generally been reaped among the poor.
V. 10, p. 433

If we see that gross error is rampant in a church, and we join its membership, we are partakers of its sins, and we will have to share in its punishment in the day of visitation.
V. 18, p. 362

How precious the church must be to the Lord when it is said he will rejoice over her with singing.
V. 44, p. 597

As the love of a husband to his bride, such is the love of Christ to his people; else the Song of Solomon means nothing at all, and is an idle book.
V. 44, p. 597

We have seen that the church has many faults—many faults— but Jesus Christ loves her and she is his bride, and I dare not find fault with her.
V. 60, p. 116

When we joined the church we were told very plainly in the Scripture that there would be tares among the wheat.
V. 60, p. 116

If some hypocrites do intrude among us, it should not astonish us.
V. 60, p. 116

COMMON SENSE
∾

We have in the Bible a book of Proverbs and another Ecclesiastes, with little spiritual teaching in them, but a great deal of good, sound, practical common sense.
V. 28, p. 209

May God, of rich mercy, give you even a little common sense, for surely, common sense would drive you to him.
V. 42, p. 142

There is nothing here on earth that is worth a man's pursuit except his God.
V. 41, p. 3

Faith in Christ is nothing but common sense sanctified of God.
V. 45, p. 283

COMMUNION
ॐ

Plunge yourself into the Godhead's deepest sea and be lost in his immensity; you shall never so fully and so truly find yourself as when you have lost yourself in God.
V. 45, p. 463

He speaks to the heart of each man in his own mother tongue, so that the miracle of Pentecost is repeated in our fellowship with Jesus.
V. 36, p. 513

There is no reason, except in ourselves, why fellowship with Jesus should not continue throughout an entire life.
V. 18, p. 91

Are you really such a stranger to God, that unless he enters into explanations you are afraid that he is not dealing fairly with you?
V. 42, p. 141

A child of God should not leave his bedroom in the morning without being on good terms with God.
V. 35, p. 335

CONFESSION
ॐ

Only on the footing of sin daily confessed and pardoned can there be any fellowship between us and the eternal God this side of heaven, for that footing is the only one consistent with the facts of the case.
V. 21, p. 362

Know this: ten thousand confessions, if they do not spring from really contrite hearts, shall be only additions to their guilt.
V. 11, p. 414

If you are conscious of impenitence, go to the Lord and tell him you have a hard heart, which will not feel either the terrors of the law or the meltings of his love: go to him just as you are, and confess what you are.
V. 21, p. 366

We will daily cry to the strong for strength, and what is prayer for strength but a confession of weakness caused by sin.
V. 21, p. 367

He will meet you where the truth is and nowhere else; when you confess that you are unworthy of his pity, you are owning the truth, and when you feel guilty, you feel what is really fact; on this footing of truth, sad truth though it be, the Lord will meet you through the atoning blood.
V. 21, p. 368

CONFLICT

Though the lions shall one day lie down with the lamb, the flesh will never agree with the spirit.
V. 25, p. 69

As the Lord has war with Amalek forever and ever; so there is war between the spirit and the flesh so long as the two are in the man.
V. 25, p. 69

The Bible does not say that you will have peace with the devil, or peace with the flesh or peace with the world; but it does say you will have peace with God.
V. 25, p. 69

We cannot mix in politics in any degree, with the purest desire for our country's welfare, without breathing a tainted air; and feel that we are on treacherous ground.
V. 27, p. 26

If you were bidden to fight a battle and were told, "God will be with you in the battle" would that be a reason why you should not fight?
V. 40, p. 78

CONSCIENCE

It is an awful thing when a man is no longer conscious of shame, but a more awful thing where he glories in his shame.
V. 24, p. 632

Conscience is a faculty of the mind which, like every other, has suffered serious damage through our natural depravity, and it is by no means perfect.
V. 19, p. 74

Conscience can only be satisfied if God is satisfied; until I see how the law is vindicated, my troubled conscience can never find rest.
V. 40, p. 31

A guilty conscience is the back door to hell.
V. 31, p. 668

CONTENTMENT

We need not teach people to complain; they complain fast enough without any education.
M. & E., p. 94

Contentment is one of the flowers of heaven and if we would have it, it must be cultivated; it will not grow in us by nature.
M. & E., p. 94

The heathen misrepresent God by worshipping idols; we misrepresent God by our murmurings and complainings.
V. 35, p. 126

Nothing is so convincing to ungodly men as to see Christians very calm in time of danger, very resigned in the hour of affliction and very patient under provocation.
V. 55, p. 606

My soul has a greater inner gladness in her deep despondency than the godless have in their high foaming merriments.
V. 23, p. 188

Our sickness is better than the worldling's health.
V. 28, p. 188

Our abasement is better than the sinner's honours.
V. 28, p. 188

We will take God at all the discount you can put upon him, and you shall have the world and all the compound interest which you are able to get out of such a sham.
V. 28, p. 188

To live means, to be in health, to be in vigour, to be in force, to be in joy, to be in right and fit condition, to have one's self in order, and to enjoy all that surrounds you with all that is within you.
V. 31, p. 676

God does not promise that he will help you who manufacture your own troubles.
V. 44, p. 468

It is true blessedness, a little heaven begun below, when the Christian, looking all around, can say of all temporal things, "I have enough."
V. 47, p. 378

It is a very different thing to be a child of God, and to have enough, and to be a child of the devil and to have enough.
V. 47, p. 379

It is an awful contentment when man can be satisfied without God.
V. 47, p. 376

What a shame it will be if those who have the grace of God within them, should fall short of the contentment which worldly men have attained.
V. 47, p. 374

CONVERSION
❦

Do not expect that every pious feeling will end in conversion.
V. 18, p. 132

Men have pretended to conversion because they hoped that a religious profession would benefit their business, or raise their social position, but from such conversions may God deliver us.
V. 19, p. 703

They may tell us there are no miracles now–a–days, but to each Christian his own conversion is a conspicuous miracle.
V. 20. p. 350

It is the rarest thing under heaven for a man who has long been a liar ever to be converted.
V. 26, p. 64

For the most part there is a sort of honest openness and freedom from trickery about those whom the Lord calls to himself.
V. 26, p. 64

Zaccheus had a curiosity to see the man Jesus Christ; the motive is not sinful, though certainly not virtuous; yet it has often been proved that curiosity is one of the best allies of grace.
V. 2, p. 73

Our converts are worth nothing: if they are converted by man they can be unconverted by man.
V. 51, p. 54

It is not light that the blind man needs, it is eyes; and eyes must be given to you who are spiritually blind if you are ever to see God.
V. 41, p. 434

Conversion may take place in a second of time and so may restoration.
V. 41, p. 440

Creation is the prerogative of Jehovah, and none can share it with him; so is it in the regeneration of a soul, instrumentality is used but the real work is immediately of the Spirit of God.
V. 31, p. 150

The child of God is of triple nature—he is spirit, soul and body: other men are duplex—body and soul.
V.17, p. 383

The joy, the gladness, the rhapsody, the exaltation in the heart of the newborn convert, is the nearest thing to paradise that earth ever saw.
V. 45, p. 475

I thought I could have leaped from earth to heaven in one spring when I first saw my sins drowned in the Redeemer's blood.
V. 45, p. 475

Trusting in Jesus Christ has changed me so completely that I scarce know my former self.
V. 15, p. 282

CONVICTION

Thou blessed Spirit, what greater curse could you inflict upon us than to leave us alone?
V. 20, p. 17

Every time a blasphemer opens his mouth to deny the truth of revelation, he will help to confirm us in our conviction of the very truth he denies.
V. 43, p. 421

I mention the oft-repeated saying of Whitefield; "If an unregenerate man could enter heaven, he would be so unhappy that he would ask God to let him run down into hell for shelter."
V. 1, p. 155, 156

Deeper than any plow can go, conviction goes to the very core and center of the spirit; till the whole heart is wounded.
V. 12, p. 86

If you feel you are desperately bad, remember you are worse than you think you are.
V. 21, p. 368

There are hundreds and thousands of men who have all that their hearts could wish, and yet they are miserable.
V. 25, p. 460

The more walking in the light there is, the clearer will be the perception of every speck and stain in the character.
V. 41, p. 18

The Holy Spirit must convince us of sin or we cannot be saved.
V. 29, p. 126

We believe and are sure, that there is such a thing as conviction of sin, and pardon for sin, both of these things are to us matters of fact.
V. 44, p. 293

If there is within your spirit a burning longing to be reconciled to God by the death of his Son, your cure is already half wrought.
V. 30, p. 436

Today we have many built up who were never pulled down, many filled who were never emptied, many exalted who were never humbled.
V. 29, p. 126

The Spirit of God comes to convince men of sin, because they never will be convinced of sin apart from his divine advocacy.
V. 29, p. 126

When the Spirit of God makes a man see sin in its naked deformity, he is horrified.
V. 29, p. 127

There is no despair that is more deep than the despair of one who was once quite secure and even boastful and self-righteous.
V. 61, p. 428

If you dare not think about your state, be sure there is something wrong with it.
V. 36, p. 431

A man truly awakened by the Spirit of God feels the remembrance of his sin to sting him as with scorpions.
V. 39, p. 183

That comfort which does not come from truth, and from God's word applied by the Holy Spirit, is a comfort to be rejected with scorn.
V. 44, p. 327

COUNTERFEIT FAITH

If you profess to be a Christian, yet find full satisfaction in worldly pleasures and pursuits, your profession is false.
M. & E., p. 355

Perhaps not a single one of you would accept the title [of atheist], and yet, if you live from Monday morning to Saturday night in the same way as you would if there were no God, you are a practical atheist.
V. 35, p. 451

Too many churchgoers are merely the stolid, unthinking, slumbering worshippers of an unknown God.
V. 11, p. 496

Vain will it be if you have listened to the most faithful of preachers, and have not listened to the preacher's Master and obeyed his gospel.
V. 26, p. 404

There are some that are the enemies of the cross of Christ and yet they have entered into the church, to her dishonour and injury.
V. 23, p. 33

There are none so bad as those who once seemed to be good.
V. 10, p. 91

Common sense teaches you, that it is not to begin, but to continue to the end which marks the genuine child of God.
V. 10, p. 91

There is a method by which a man may attain to a great reputation as a Christian and yet avoid all the trials of the believer's estate.
V. 10, p. 365

We are encumbered with a host of people who call themselves Christians, but we are as much of the world as other people who are altogether of the world.
V. 25, p. 490

The whole of some men's religion is a kind of sleepwalking, void of vigour and earnestness.
V. 27, p. 641

When a man once convinces himself to play the double, both to fear God and serve other gods, he is very apt to stick there.
V. 27, p. 565

If you must speculate let it be with your gold; but I plead with you, venture not with your immortal spirit.
V. 44, p. 296

On the anvil of false profession Satan hammers out the most hardened of hearts.
V. 27, p. 565

If I am in a condition in which I dare not meet my God, may God in mercy fetch me out of that condition at once.
V. 27, p. 568

O you religious worldlings, for you there is reserved the blackness of darkness forever.
V. 27, p. 564

That religion which will not stand the test of all weathers is worth nothing.
V. 40, p. 46

We have a lot of sham sinners about, and we have ministers who preach a sham saviour, and a sham salvation; and the sham sinners like to have it so.
V. 30, p. 489

Wherever there is a true child of God there will be concern
for his family: If you do not want your children saved, you are
not saved yourself.
V. 13, p. 407

Any kind of faith in Christ which does not change your life is
the faith of devils, and will take you where devils are, but will
never take you to heaven.
V. 60, p. 40

If faith does not produce good works, it is a dead faith.
V. 60, p. 40

If you have a hope in the mercy of God, which lets you do
what the ungodly do with impunity, you have about your
neck a mill-stone that will sink you lower than the lowest hell.
V. 60, p. 40 & 41

I have seen scores of men jump into religion just as men jump
into a bath, and then jump out again just as quickly.
V. 60, p. 42

There is no sound bottom to a man's religion unless he begins
with a broken heart.
V. 60, p. 42

Beware of trusting in your prayers, or your Bible reading, in
your hymns and holy thoughts and almsgivings; they are all
lighter than vanity.
V. 45, p. 282

Beware if that Christianity from which Christ has been eliminated.
V. 46, p. 544

Many are criticizing, and amusing themselves, and while pro-
fessing everything, are believing nothing.
V. 36, p. 507

Many are in the visible church who do not belong to God.
V. 36, p. 429

That which you do because you are afraid to act otherwise is
no evidence of a changed heart.
V. 47, p. 46

There are many, who know nothing of vital godliness, yet who sing as joyfully as the brightest of saints, never suspecting their real condition before God.
V. 50, p. 93

I would sooner you had no religion and made no pretense to have any, than to have the imitation of it.
V. 31, p. 444

Shall saints be shams when sinners are so real.
V. 31, p. 444

In proportion as the privilege and honour of a child of God is great, the sin of false pretensions to grace is increased.
V. 18, p. 15

God save us from making a profession if we have not the grace to live up to it.
V. 18, p. 16

Every precious thing in this world is sure to be counterfeited.
V. 36, p. 422

We have many round about us, who can talk of heaven and hell and sin and salvation and Christ and the Holy Spirit who have never had one true perception of the meaning of these words.
V. 39, p. 182

CREATION

In the beginning God created the heaven and the earth; then came a long interval, and at length, at the appointed time, during seven days, the Lord prepared the earth for the human race.
V. 17, p. 377

DEATH
✑

God will not give men an immortality in this life to spend in disregarding him, they must die.
V. 30, p. 191

Men may put Christ far from them, but they cannot put death far from them; they may avoid the cross but they cannot avoid the grave.
V. 30, p. 191

We are speeding onwards through our brief life like an arrow shot from a bow, and we feel that we shall not drop down at the end of our flight into the dreariness of annihilation; but we shall find a heavenly target far across the flood of death.
V. 5, p. 393

The best moment of a Christian's life is his last one, because it is the one nearest heaven.
V. 58, p. 600

You are not going to a land of toil and poverty, sorrow and death; you are going to be forever with the Lord where no evil can reach you.
V. 34, p. 463

Your death-day shall be your heavenly wedding-day, and your last day on earth shall be the best day you ever spent on it.
V. 34, p. 464

Some children of God are always delighted at the idea that Christ may come and that they shall never die: I would be delighted if the Lord should come at once; but as to dying or not dying I do not care a jot.
V. 34, p. 465

In death the financial element looks contemptible, and the moral and spiritual come to be the most esteemed.
V. 23, p. 508

Death finds out the truth of our condition and blows away with his cold breath a heap of chaff which we thought to be good wheat.
V. 23, p. 509

Dying men want realities, they want a sinner's Saviour, they want atonement for guilt, for so only can they pass out of the world with hope.
V. 25, p. 509

Life is so short that we have scarce begin to live when we are called to die.
V. 23, p. 509

There are some who will be "alive and remain" at the coming of the Lord, but is there so very much advantage in such an escape from death as to make it the object of Christian desire?
T. D. Vol. 1, p. 401

I think that of the two, it might be preferable to die, because those who die will have a kind of fellowship with Christ in his death which will not be experienced by those who never sleep in the tomb.
V. 34, p. 465

A sister used to be much troubled about dying; she knew where she was going but she dreaded the passage: she died in her sleep and in all probability never knew when she passed away and found herself among the angels.
V. 35, p. 262

Nothing on earth ever gives me so much establishment in the faith as to visit members of this church when they are about to die.
V. 35, p. 262

To be prepared to die is to be prepared to live; to be ready for eternity is, in the best sense, to be ready for time.
V. 23, p. 512

Let us be of Paul's mind when he said, "to die is gain" and "to depart and be with Christ is far better."
T. D. Vol. 1, p. 401

How joyous it is to be weaned from the world, and to ready
to depart from it; to be with Christ is far better than to tarry
in this vale of tears.
V. 10, p. 187

We are not afraid of the day of judgment because we have
peace with God, and hence we are not afraid to die.
V. 25, p. 71

Death to the saint is the gate of endless joy, and shall he
dread to enter there?
V. 25, p. 463

In proportion as your faith gets stronger, your fear of death
will vanish, and as your faith gets weak, fear will come in to
take its place.
V. 55, p. 10

Death is the end of dying; on the day of the believer's death
dying is forever done with.
V. 27, p. 155

Death is the last enemy, and turns out to be the death of
every enemy.
V. 27, p. 155

To die by your own hand is not to escape from suffering, but
to plunge yourself into it forever.
V. 51, p. 16

He that murders himself, if he knows what he is doing, gives
sure evidence that eternal life is not in him.
V. 51, p. 16

Paul said, "I die daily," if we die every day, it will not be hard
to die on our last day.
V. 44, p. 462

We have a very clear conviction that others will die, but as to
ourselves, we put far from us the evil day.
V. 30, p. 182

Death is an awful thing to those who have their all in this world.
V. 30, p. 182

Count for me all the gold that could buy this round world, yet would I not accept it if I must live in fear of death.
V. 30, p. 191

Believers have everything to gain by dying: "to die is gain," we shall lose nothing which will be a loss to us.
V. 30, p. 192

Some of our most earnest helpers have passed away; but it has been a pleasure and a privilege to see them rejoicing while everybody else was weeping.
V. 44, p. 295

Give me a religion by which I can live, for that is the religion on which I can die.
V. 44, p. 295

There is a power beyond ourselves which has made us sublimely calm when we have seemed to stand between the open jaws of death.
V. 44, p. 292

Life is a blessing because after life comes death which is the gateway to endless joy.
V. 44, p. 462

We have every now and then expressed a longing to depart: not so much, I fear, because of our eagerness to be with Christ, but because we have grown weary with the trials and sufferings of this poor wilderness.
V. 60, p. 325

Are you afraid of dying? never be afraid of that; be afraid of living: living is the only thing which can do any mischief.
V. 45, p. 275

Death is emancipation, deliverance, heavens bliss to a child of God.
v 45, p. 276

Can he ever be an infidel who has seen his mother die joyful-ly triumphant?
V. 45, p. 281

We shall not be afraid of the messenger of death, for we shall regard him as an angel of the covenant sent to fetch God's people up to heaven.
V. 46, p. 537

Some of us know what it is to gaze on death, and we have grown so used to the prospect, and so peaceful in reference to it, that we have almost been sorry to come back again to life with its trials and sins.
V. 36, p. 511

When we were so prepared and even jubilant in the prospect of passing into the world of spirits, we almost reluctantly turned our face earthward again.
V. 36, p. 511

Gold is nothing but dust to a dying man.
V. 36, p. 524

Man has an inborn conscience that he is not to be extin-guished by death.
V. 32, p. 13

I would gladly die a million deaths to see him as he is and to be like him.
V. 22, p. 31

Though he permits his saints to lay down their lives for his sake, yet not one life is spent in vain, or unnecessarily expended.
V. 18, p. 97

If it were in our power to confer immortality upon our beloved Christian brethren and sisters we would surely do it, and to their injury we would detain them here in this wilderness.
V. 18, p. 98

Grievous are their deaths in our sight, but precious are their deaths in his sight (Ps. 116:15)
V. 18, p. 98

Tears are permitted to us, but they must glisten in the light of faith and hope.
V. 18, p. 98

Jesus wept, but Jesus never repined.
V. 18, p. 98

To the saints the sting of death is gone; it is no more a penalty but a privilege to die.
V. 18, p. 99

When Baxter lay dying the last word he said was in answer to the question "How are you?" "Almost well," said he, and so it was.
V. 18, p. 101

When God says that the death of a believer is precious in his sight, it is clear that no tinge of annihilation is in the idea, for where would be the preciousness of a believer ceasing to exist.
V. 18, p. 100

Precious to Jehovah is the death of the least in the ranks, as the death of those who rush to the front and bear the brunt of the battle.
V. 18, p. 102

After death our thoughts, our cares, our desires, our joys, will all be in God.
V. 14, p. 657

In your departing moments you shall have most extraordinary grace; with joyful heart you shall sing, "O death where is your sting."
V. 14, p. 237

We all count all men mortal but ourselves.
V. 42, p. 135

Death to the sinner is a curse, but to the believer it is a form of benediction, it is the gate of life.
V. 39, p. 50

When the rich man has made his fortune, he wins six foot of earth, and nothing more, and what less has he who was a pauper.
V. 12, p. 640

When you are fit to suffer, and if needs be to die, Christ will not screen you from so high an honor.
V. 12, p. 652

Jesus Christ did not come to give you comfort while you are under the fear of death, but he came to deliver those who through fear of death are all their lifetime subject to bondage.
V. 12, p. 359

If the very thought of death is bitter, what will the reality be for reckless sinners?
V. 11, p. 342

What do we live for, if it is not to prepare for the life hereafter and for the day for which all days were made?
V. 11, p. 347

Death is the gate to endless joy; and do we dread to enter there?
V. 44, p. 462

DEPRAVITY

You who are so fair to look upon when you look in the glass of your self–adulation, if you could see yourself as God sees you, would discover that you are leprous from head to foot.
V. 19, p. 678

A beast would scarcely become so evil and vile as human nature becomes when it is left alone fully to develop itself.
V. 21, p. 88

The treatment of our Lord Jesus Christ by men is the clearest proof of total depravity which can possibly be discovered.
V. 34, p. 473

Evil things are easy things for they are natural to our fallen nature but right things are rare flowers that need cultivation.
V. 34, p. 473

Is it not a sad proof of the alienation of our nature that
though God is everywhere we have to school ourselves to
perceive him anywhere?
V. 22, p. 411

You know nothing about conversion if you merely believe in
human depravity, but have never felt that you are depraved
and that you yourself are ruined.
V. 13, p. 638

That he must be nailed to a cross and die like a felon, there
must have been some awful mischief to remove.
V. 26, p. 631

Even if a man had no other sin whatsoever, it is quite sufficient to condemn him forever, if he neglects his God and
turns away from his Saviour.
V. 25, p. 267

Unbelief is an act of high treason against the divine majesty.
V. 25, p. 268

Some are graduates in the university of self–importance, full
of ignorance and equally full of pride, they refuse to give
Christ a hearing.
V. 25, p. 268

The natural man lies covered with sores at the gates of mercy,
having nothing of his own but sin, unable to dig and unwilling
to beg, and therefore perishing in a penury of the direst kind.
V. 55, p. 377

I do not think there are any men or women here who have
the slightest idea of what evil they may be capable of if they
are put under certain conditions, and the grace of God is
taken away.
V. 40, p. 45

The world is base enough to desire to slay its God even when
he comes on an errand of love.
V. 29, p. 131

Affliction might have produced in some a splendid character if all had been right to begin with; but since it was all wrong, that very process which should have ripened them into sweetness has hastened them to rottenness.
V. 27, p. 638

Some of the most outrageous blasphemers were originally Sunday–school scholars and teachers, young men who were "almost persuaded," yet they halted and hesitated, and wavered until they made the plunge and became much worse than they possibly could have become if they had not seen the light of truth.
V. 26, p. 407

Every supposed good thing that grows out of your own self, is like yourself, mortal, and it must die.
V. 17, p. 382

That slow–burning smoldering fire called malice is nearest akin to the fire of hell.
V. 25, p. 461

Let my right hand forget her cunning ere I shall begin to preach about the dignity of human nature, and the grandeur of the miserable wretch called man.
V. 45, p. 466

If I search myself and my whole life over and over again, I cannot see anything but what I call filthy rags.
V. 47, p. 29

When you have a sense of being the greatest of sinners, remember you are a greater sinner than you think yourself to be.
V. 36, p. 89

If you were now in hell, you would have no cause to complain against the justice of God, for you deserve to be there.
V. 36, p. 89

The sin that lies within us is not an accumulation of external defilement, but an inward all–pervading corruption.
V. 28, p. 605

Are there not many who wish that fornication and adultery were not vices, proving that their hearts are depraved?
V. 28, p. 607

He is not a less sinner, but a greater sinner who being born in the midst of godliness, ventures to depart from the good way.
V. 28, p. 175

Men by nature do not give dominion to their nobler part, but allow the brute in them to overrule the mind.
V. 37, p. 14

The apostle does not say that the carnal mind is at enmity, but he gives us the solid noun: he says, "the carnal mind is enmity against God."
V. 32, p. 14

If you are not born again from above, I am compelled to say, even the best of you, that your fleshly mind is enmity against God.
V. 32, p. 15

Because of the fall and man's depravity, justice now comes in with its rod and sword and changes the complexion of our life.
V. 24, p. 61

You that think yourselves the biggest, blackest sinners do not think so badly of yourselves as I often think and rightly think of myself.
V. 24, p. 70

The doctrine of the depravity of the human race is not merely an article in the creed; it is a matter of everyday experience.
V. 50, p. 353

Human nature is depraved, and therefore there must be an extraordinary pressure of the Holy Spirit put upon the heart to lead us to ask for mercy.
V. 4, p. 339

Until a man sees Christ he walks in darkness and is stone blind and beholds no light.
V. 15, p. 306

There is nothing that the worst of men have done which the best of men could not do if they were left by the grace of God.
V. 39, p. 89

DILIGENCE
℘

Nobody is good by accident, no man ever became holy by chance.
V. 32, p. 79

It is a very bad thing for anyone when even the Christian life gets to be merely mechanical.
V. 44, p. 99

We are expected to use all available means, we are not allowed to be idle and do nothing, because we say we are trusting in providence.
V. 44, p. 110

If I wish to be a man of learning, I cannot get it simply by praying for it; I must study, even to the weariness of the flesh.
V. 44, p. 110

There is no stronger and more forceful principle for fetching out the energy of a man than his conviction that God is with him.
V. 44, p. 110

He will clothe you with rags if you clothe yourself with idleness.
V. 44, p. 111

Feel the weight of men's souls till it crushes you down to Christ's feet, but do not let it crush you down any lower than that; you are not the saviour, you are not to have the glory of their salvation.
V. 44, p. 119

Many stumble into the bottomless pit with their eyes shut, but no man ever yet entered into heaven by a leap in the dark.
V. 44, p. 26

DIVINE LEADING

Has he who made you launched you forth on the tempestuous sea of life without compass or guide?
V. 61, p. 181

If any man desires to act according to the mind of God, light will come to him sooner or later.
V. 47, p. 27

No man, who acts honestly up to the light he has, will be left in the dark.
V. 47, p. 27

DOCTRINE

A man says, "I am not a Calvinist nor an Armenian, nor a Baptist nor a Presbyterian, nor an Independent;" he follows himself and so belongs to the smallest denomination in the world.
V. 11, p. 631

My dear hearers, I do not ask you to believe anything I say, because I say it; fling it to the wind if it has no better authority than mine.
V. 11, p. 631

We should, as a rule, treat heresy as ignorance to be enlightened rather than as a crime to be condemned, unless it becomes willful perversity.
V. 23, p. 18

We know some in whom the slightest variation from their system arouses their indignation.
V. 23, p. 687

True doctrine is to us priceless as a throne for our living Lord, but our chief delight is not in the vacant throne but in the king's presence thereon.
V. 23, p. 687

Truth isolated from the person of Jesus grows hard and cold.
V. 23, p. 687

Do not trifle away your soul by thrusting your head into doctrinal difficulties.
V. 14, p. 352

He who is altogether and only a Calvinist probably only knows half the truth, but he who is willing to take the other side as far as it is true and believing all he finds in the Word, will get the whole pearl.
V. 61, p. 115

DREAMS

What could there be to assure the soul of its salvation in the vain and frolicsome motions of the mind when they are free from the bridle of reason.
V. 16, p. 315

Dreams may sometimes happen to come true, but nine times out of ten they are nonsense.
V. 16, p. 315

It would be a dreadful thing to hang one's confidence on such a fragile thing as a dream.
V. 16, p. 315

ELECTION

There is no doctrine in Scripture more humbling than that of election, none more promotive of gratitude, and consequently none more sanctifying.
M. & E., p. 661

Electing love has selected some of the worst to be made the best.
M. & E., p. 684

I do chose God most freely, most fully, but it must be because
of some previous work in my heart, changing that heart; for
my unrenewed heart never would have chosen him.
V. 10, p. 489

If men turn their backs on heaven's everflowing fountain,
shall they afterwards quarrel with the election of God because
he causes some to come whom he makes willing in the day of
his power.
V. 27, p. 8 & 9

Many persons want to know their election before they look to
Christ but they cannot because it is only discovered by look-
ing to Jesus.
M. & E., p. 398

My nature is in itself so adverse to this way of salvation that, if
I really and from my heart accepted it, there must have been an
operation on my heart from God to bring me to this condition.
V. 40, p. 536

If you tremble at God's Word, you have one of the surest
marks of God's elect.
V. 35, p. 311

They do not pray for themselves; poor ignorant souls, they do
not know anything about prayer; but Jesus prays for them.
V. 10, p. 102

No curse falls upon these; they deserve it, but the eternal love
prevents it; they may well perish because they seek not mercy,
but Christ intercedes for them, and live they shall.
V. 10, p. 102

We know of some who have imagined themselves to be elect
because of the visions they have seen; these are as much
value as cobwebs would be for a garment.
V. 51, p. 53

The gospel is preached in the ears of all; it only comes with
power to some.
V. 51, p. 54

We might preach until we should exhaust our lungs and die,
but never a soul would be converted unless there were the
mysterious power of the Holy Spirit going with it.
V. 51, p. 54

Your evidence of election is blotted and blurred unless the
Word has come to you with demonstration of the Spirit and
with power.
V. 51, p. 55

The Lord help you to trust Jesus and then you may go on
your way with joy, knowing your election of God.
V. 51, p. 59

The omnipotent grace of God exerts itself in a way and manner suitable to the free agency of human beings, so that grace
gets the victory, but at the same time, a man acts as a man.
V. 46, p. 545

If in your heart you confess that you deserve condemnation,
you are the kind of person that God chose before the foundation of the world.
V. 36, p. 93

If you have looked to Christ, it is because Christ has looked at
you and influenced you to look to him.
V. 32, p. 497

What a wonder it is that men and women who had never
thought about God should nevertheless be turned into seekers.
V. 32, p. 502

Sinner, cast away your despondency—may you not be elect as
well as any other? for there is a host innumerable chosen.
V. 1, p. 322

Men do not seek God first; God seeks them first and if any of
you are seeking him today it is because he has first sought you.
V. 4, p. 339

The only reason why any man ever begins to pray, is because
God has put previous grace in his heart which leads him to pray.
V. 4, p. 339

Election is based upon affection and that affection is its own fountain.
V. 33, p. 507

There have been men at work or at their amusements, in their wickedness, who have had impressions which have made them new men when it was least expected such a thing would occur.
V. 14, p. 154

The sovereign electing grace of God chooses us to repentance, to faith and afterwards to holiness of living.
V. 14, p. 351

Let us never think about proving our election unless we bring forth fruit unto holiness by the grace of God.
V. 14, p. 351

There will always be some who will pervert and wrest this doctrine to their own destruction.
V. 14, p. 352

Long before the minister is sent to preach the gospel, God prepares the hearts of men to receive the Word.
V. 14, p. 353

Your present business is with the precept which is revealed, not with election which is concealed.
V. 11, p. 607

Your responsibility is not with metaphysical difficulty but with faith in the atonement of the Lord Jesus Christ, which is simple and plain enough.
V. 11, p. 607

Man has a free will, yes and God has a free will too; and when those two come into conflict, it is God's free will that wins the day.
V. 43, p. 438

Those whom he has determined to bless will be blessed, whatever the devil may say to the contrary.
V. 43, p. 438

An extortion to men is not inconsistent with the strongest doctrine of grace, the decree of God in no sense renders the effort of man unnecessary.

V. 43, p. 440

If there is anything that makes believers hearts sing unto the Lord, it is the recollection that he has chosen them, and fixed his love upon them.

V. 44, p. 589

ENVY

Many a hero of truth has been despised for the very reason which ought to have secured him honour.

V. 25, p. 90

How can you feel the miseries of envy when you possess in Christ the best of all portions?

V. 15, p. 222

ETERNAL LIFE

The certainty of our eternal life is proven by the certainty of Christ's death.

V. 26, p. 632

It would not be life to our souls to know God apart from his son, Jesus Christ.

V. 41, p. 31

I have an immortal spark which cannot have been intended to burn on this poor earth, and then go out; it must have been meant to burn on heaven's altar.

V. 11, p. 131

The flesh dies but the new nature which God gives us is immortal as God himself; it can neither be quenched here by temptation, nor there by the act of death.

V. 11, p. 644

EVOLUTION

Men of progress care nothing for evolution in itself, but only so far as it may serve their purpose of escaping from the thought of God.
V. 32, p. 495

These philosopher speculators believe that this big world, and the sun and moon and stars came forth without a creator: they can believe anything.
V. 18, p. 58

You cannot convince the simplest boy in the street that some-how or other he developed from an oyster, and yet these pro-found thinkers bow themselves down to such a belief as this.
V. 18, p. 58

EXPERIENCE

If the price of which you shall have a true experience is that of sorrow, buy the truth at that price.
V. 61, p. 114

Let us set our heart upon this, that we mean to have, by God's help, all that the infinite goodness of God is ready to bestow.
V. 28, p. 303

Expect that, if God promised you anything, he will be true to his word; but, beyond that, do not expect anything beneath the moon.
V. 50, p. 356

FAITH

To describe creation without a Creator, design without a Designer, is to fly from the difficulties of faith to the impossi-bilities of unbelief.
V. 35, p. 666

A man is saved by faith alone without works, and yet no man can be saved by a faith that is without works?
V. 48, p. 222

If I say that I believe in God and yet continue to live in sin, willfully and knowingly, then I have not so good a faith as the devils have, for they "believe and tremble."
V. 48, p. 222

Look back, believer, and note that to you the existence of God has not been a theory, but a fact observed and verified by actual experience.
V. 20, p. 350

I think it more to my soul's benefit to believe than to understand, for faith brings me nearer to God than reason ever did.
V. 33, p. 199

Understanding would compel me to keep to the shallows, but faith takes me to the main ocean.
V. 33, p. 199

The grandeur of the arch of heaven would be spoiled if the sky were supported by a single visible column, and your faith would lose its glory if it rested on anything discernible by the carnal eye.
M. & E., p. 488

It is faith that saves us, not works, but the faith that saves us always produces works.
V. 21, p. 89

There may be certain reasons requiring the trial of faith, rather than the reward of faith.
V. 12, p. 567

Saving faith learns to credit contradiction to laugh at impossibilities, and to say, "It cannot be, but yet it will be."
V. 30, p. 478

Now you who have been studying the results of faith in yourselves and are dissatisfied, I beseech you turn your eyes away from yourselves and look to Jesus himself.
V. 23, p. 689

Put no confidence in the mere fact that you hold to an orthodox faith, for a dead orthodoxy soon corrupts.
V. 31, p. 118

We have no more faith at any time than we have in the hour of trial.
V. 33, p. 289

Even when faith does become developed, yet I warrant you its stature never reaches the height of the promise.
V. 21, p. 664

Beware of a faith that will not stand self–examination: if you dare not look into your own heart, it must be because there is something rotten there.
V. 39, p. 148

It seems to me a harder thing not to believe in Jesus than to believe in him, if one is indeed willing to be made whole.
V. 18, p. 45

Even prayer can only be a mockery if it be not the prayer of faith.
V. 57, p. 337

We not only begin to live by faith, but continue to live in the same manner.
V. 57, p. 337

The Holy Spirit leads us to faith, but the faith is our own act and deed.
V. 57, p. 338

The only trust that saves the soul is that practical trust which obeys Jesus Christ: faith that does not obey is dead faith.
V. 57, p. 339

Where faith does exist, it is the gift of God; but where it does not exist, it is because men will not believe in him, but shut their eyes to his light.
V. 57, p. 339

Many persons are anxious to be saved, which is a good thing;
but they have mapped out the way in which they want God to
save them, which is a bad thing.
V. 57, p. 340

Eyegate is closed, for through Eargate eternal life comes into
the soul of man: "faith comes by hearing."
V. 57, p. 340–341

Let preacher and hearer be amazed that we should ever dare
to say that we find faith in God to be difficult.
V. 55, p. 243

It is a grievous imputation upon God when we talk about
faith as hard.
V. 55, p. 243

If we should say of a neighbor, "I find it hard to believe him,"
I do not know what worse we could say of him.
V. 55, p. 243

Untried faith is questionable faith: is it faith at all?
V. 31, p. 664

Give up the hopeless effort of dragging into the mind by
efforts of reason that which can so readily dwell in you by the
Holy Spirit through faith.
V. 37, p. 49

Obedience is the natural outcome of belief.
V. 37, p. 501

The faith which justifies the soul is the gift of God and
not ourselves.
V. 17, p. 380

Certain Christians are afraid that they cannot be saved because
they are not joyous but we are saved by faith, not by joy.
V. 27, p. 77

There is no living with peace and joy of the Holy Spirit in
the heart, if we wander from the simplicity of our confidence
in Christ.
V. 61, p. 163

If faith is slain, where is love, where is hope, where is repentance?
V. 45, p. 208

The victory is virtually won by the arch–enemy if he is able to conquer faith, for faith is the noble chief among the graces.
V. 45, p. 208

The devil will not trouble himself so much about your other graces, he will probably attack them when he can; but first of all he says, "Down with faith."
V. 45, p. 209

Satan knows it is the thing which most of all helps to overthrow his kingdom; therefore, believer, cling to your faith!
V. 45, p. 209

It is not a vain thing for me to believe in Christ; it is my life, it is my strength, it is my joy.
V. 45, p. 211

Wherever faith exists, it is the gift of God; it is a plant that never sprang up spontaneously from the soil of corrupt human nature.
V. 45, p. 241

I know of no cause of disquietude that faith cannot remove.
V. 45, p. 280

It is one thing to believe a general doctrine, but it is quite another to make a particular and personal application of it.
V. 46, p. 229

If you would grow in faith, you must live near the cross.
V. 46, p. 536

To believe is to take freely what God gives freely.
V. 36, p. 502

We need faith for buying, for selling, for working, quite as much as for praying, and singing, and preaching.
V. 36, p. 303

Only that is true faith which believes everything that is revealed by the Holy Spirit, whether it be joyous or distressing.
V. 36, p. 303

We would be humble, and learn to believe what we cannot comprehend.
V. 36, p. 304

It is our ambition to be child–like in faith rather than subtle in intellect.
V. 36, p. 304

My Lord gives me unlimited credit at the bank of faith.
V. 36, p. 95

Trusting in the Lord is simply depending where there is unquestionable reason for reliance.
V. 24, p. 711

Men cannot even understand what trusting in the Lord means until the Holy Spirit opens their understanding.
V. 24, p. 712

Strong faith is well content with the Lord's settled and usual mode of action.
V. 24, p. 383

An abyss immeasurable yawns between the man who has even the smallest faith in Christ and the man who has none.
V. 36, p. 613

Strong faith is content without signs, without tokens, without marvels; it believes God's bare word and asks for no confirming miracle.
V. 36, p. 615

Strong faith takes Jesus only as her basis; but feeble faith tries to add thereto.
V. 36, p. 617

If you say of God's promises, "I can believe some of them and therefore I expect him to help me under certain difficulties" you are accusing the Lord of unfaithfulness.
V. 36, p. 618

If you have weak faith you will have broken joys and many discomforts.
V. 36, p. 618

Go learn to plead on when no answer comes and to press on when repulsed: this is the test of faith.
V. 33, p. 282

Even you that have believed and are saved are not half as sure as you ought to be.
V. 28, p. 69

There is a kind of faith which is strong in one direction, but utter weakness if tried in other ways.
V. 28, p. 644

I trusted Jesus and I lived: I gave up trying to understand, I believed and I lived.
V. 32, p. 502

Trust is the simplicity of a babe, but it is the glory of a genius.
V. 24, p. 714

Faith in the storm is true faith; faith in the calm may or may not be true faith.
V. 50, p. 361

Genuine faith believes anything and everything the Lord says whether discouraging or encouraging.
V. 22, p. 461

Faith that humbly links itself to Christ has in it as great beauty as the rainbow.
V. 16, p. 337

Do not imagine that to have faith in Christ you have to work yourselves up into the idea that there is some good thing in you which can recommend you to Christ.
V. 16, p. 347

Faith is to credit contradictions, and believe in impossibilities.
V. 33, p. 272

I ought to be afraid of presumption, but it cannot be presumptuous to believe God's word.
V. 18, p. 69

Faith justifies, but not in and by itself, but because it grasps the obedience of Christ.
V. 14, p. 677

Faith must look to the atonement and work of Jesus, or else it is not the faith of Scripture.
V. 14, p. 677

I do not wonder that your faith grows weak when you fail to consider the tremendous sacrifice which Jesus made for his people.
V. 14, p. 682

Contemplate once again the wondrous transaction of substitution and you will find your faith revived.
V. 14, p. 682

Little faith must have everything very plain or else it cannot move at all; but great faith makes crooked things straight, sees light in the midst of darkness, and gathers comfort out of discouragement.
V. 42, p. 2

Full assurance is the proper tone of an educated faith.
V. 42, p. 111

I do no think that we are at all lacking in confidence in ourselves; but it is in confidence in God that is wanted, and that is quite another thing.
V. 42, p. 113

Faith is a grand support for courage and steadfastness.
V. 43, p. 524

When I listened to George Müller, some years ago, I do not think there was very much in what he said if I took the words apart from himself, but with that holy blessed life of faith at the back of every word I was like a child sitting at a tutor's feet to learn from him.
V. 43, p. 128

No faith is so precious as that which triumphs over adversity.
M. & E., 634

Our Lord is very discriminating; he distinguishes between faith and presumption, and between faith and our idea of faith.
V. 38, p. 409

FEAR OF GOD

There is no greater coward in this world than the man who will never own that he is afraid.
V. 57, p. 268

There is a kind of fear which we have need to cultivate, for it leads to repentance and confession of sin, to aspirations after holiness, and to the utter rejection of all self–complacency and self–conceit.
V. 48, p. 497

The more we fear the Lord the more we love him, until this becomes to us the true fear of God, to love him with all our heart and soul and strength.
V. 48, p. 498

I fear lest I should grieve him by anything that looks like ingratitude.
V. 48, p. 500

Worldlings may well be afraid, for they have an angry God above them, a guilty conscience within them and a yawing hell beneath them.
M. & E., p. 227

We are filled with fear at times on purpose that our religion may not be a flimsy, superficial thing.
V. 13, p. 250

The fear of God is the death of every other fear.
V. 13, p. 250

Anarchy comes in when the fear of God goes out; and all the mischiefs you can imagine, and much more, rush in like a flood.
V. 35, p. 664

It is not possible that mortal men should be thoroughly conscious of the divine presence without being filled with awe.
V. 25, p. 278

It is not given to such frail creatures as we are to stand in the
full blaze of Godhead without crying out with the prophet
[Habakkuk] "I was afraid."
V. 25, p. 279

Outward religion depends upon the excitement which created
it; but the fear of the Lord lives on when all around it is
frost–bitten.
V. 27, p. 577

Fear is not a mean motive; it is a very proper motive for a
guilty man to feel.
V. 30, p. 492

Where else can such poor sinners as we are begin, except
with selfish fear?
V. 30, p. 492

Between the fear of God's great power and justice which the
devils have, and that fear which a child of God has when he
walks in the light, there is as much difference as between hell
and heaven.
V. 48, p. 496

Daniel looked into the face of his God, and would not fear
the face of a lion.
V. 14, p. 335

If your presence in the sanctuary is not a matter of your own
deliberate choice, if you do not desire to fear God's name,
there is nothing in it that is acceptable to God.
V. 47, p. 75

FEAR OF MAN
❧

Multitudes who know the truth and are not far from the kingdom of God, nevertheless never enter it, because of the fear of man, the love of approbation or the horror of being laughed at and ridiculed.
V. 26, p. 71

Never be afraid of the world's censure; its praise is much more to be dreaded.
V. 28, p. 186

There are thousands of men who have no fear of God, but who have great fear of man.
V. 54, p. 85

It was the fear of man that caused Pilate's name to become infamous in the history of the world.
V. 54, p. 87

Do you mean to fling away your immortal soul in order to escape the laughter of fools.
V. 54, p. 88

I appeal to your conscience to say if it is worth while to be eternally ruined for the sake of pleasing men?
V. 54, p. 88

Shall we lose our souls to escape the sneers of fools?
V. 61, p. 618

Surely among all cowards he is the worst who is afraid to be true to God.
V. 32, p. 491

If we are afraid of puny man how shall we be able to face it out before the dread ordeal of the judgment day?
V. 11, p. 340

FELLOWSHIP

This personal desire of the believer after God is another form of fellowship with him.

V. 41, p. 439

You will indeed have fellowship with the Father, and with his Son, when you are nothing and Christ is everything.

V. 50, p. 499

Throughout the whole Divine plan of salvation; in the purpose, in the object of that purpose, in the plan by which it is achieved, the believer in Christ has fellowship with the Father.

V. 7, p. 491

So in this then we have fellowship with the Father, seeing that we are both agreed in loving the Son.

V. 7, p. 492

Enoch's life had no adventures, is it not adventure enough to walk with God?

V. 22, p. 439

We could doubt our own existence sooner than we could doubt the supernatural presence of Christ with true believers.

V. 44, p. 292

FORGIVENESS

Of all the things in the world, I think the most loathsome and sickening is the pretense of forgiving a person when you yourself are the one who committed the offense.

V. 19, p. 203

When God laid sin upon Christ it must have been the intent of his heart that he would never lay it upon those for whom Christ died.

V. 25, p. 64

O God, you have forgiven your servants; but we have never forgiven ourselves, and we never mean to.
V. 41, p. 306

When you come to him do not ask him first to heal your souls disease, but first to forgive your sins.
V. 25, p. 497

Not "who will perhaps forgive you on your death bed," but who is now forgiving daily, hourly, momentarily, continually forgiving all your iniquities.
V. 25, p. 497

We shall grow in grace, but we shall never be more completely pardoned than when we first believed.
V. 25, p. 498

Alas, I may be sinning, for even in the holiest of deeds there is sin, but even then God is forgiving.
V. 25, p. 498

We still sin even when walking in the light and still need Jesus to cleanse us by his blood.
V. 25, p. 498

I heartily wish that I could sit down and have a happy cry over this blessed truth that my God is at this moment forgiving me.
V. 25, p. 498

Nobody ever sings over an uncertain pardon; a doubt as to your forgiveness is fatal to joy.
V. 25, p. 499

Our sense of guilt arises from our knowledge of the law, and that is clear; but our sense of forgiveness comes from our knowledge of the gospel and that is equally clear.
V. 25, p. 499

Lord, forgive all my iniquities, my good works and my bad works, I have tried to sort them a little but one is so much like the other that I fling them overboard and swim to glory in the cross.
V. 25, p. 503

If you are pardoned once you are forgiven once–for all, irreversible acquittals God bestows; for the gifts and calling of God are irrevocable.
V. 25, p. 503

Until God can change or lie, he never will bring to mind again the sin of one whom he has pardoned.
V. 25, p. 503

If you live as long as Methuselah, the transgressions of all those years are covered by the blood of Christ.
V. 25, p. 503

Many are tempted to believe that they are too great sinners for Christ to pardon; this is undervaluing the merit of Christ's blood and a denial of the truthfulness of God's promise.
V. 8, p. 400

It is high insult against the majesty of God's love when you are tempted to believe that you are beyond the mercy of God.
V. 8, p. 400

When God laid sin upon Christ it must have been the intent of his heart that he would never lay it upon those for whom Christ died.
V. 25, p. 64

O God, you have forgiven your servants; but we have never forgiven ourselves and we never intend to.
V. 41, p. 306

FREE AGENCY

The free agency of man is a self–evident truth.
V. 50, p. 350

I believe in the free agency of man as much as anyone who lives; but I equally believe in the eternal purpose of God.
V. 46, p. 174

Infinitely glorious, achieving his own purposes, not only in the world of dead, inert matter, but also through those who are free agents.

V. 46, p. 174

No real faith was ever wrought in man by his own thoughts and imaginations; he must receive the gospel as a revelation from God, or he cannot receive it at all.

V. 25, p. 269

FUTURE

What is the present, after all, but a fleeting show, an empty dream; but the future is eternal and incorruptible.

V. 46, p. 250

We know so little of the future that to worry about it would be the height of unwisdom.

V. 34, p. 666

Our view of the near future may be incorrect; why fret over that which will never happen.

V. 34, p. 666

Though the angels excel us now, we shall certainly excel them in the world to come.

V. 25, p. 186

There is no reason, because of the darkness of the past, why the future should not be bright.

V. 16, p. 339

He that enlists in the army of Christ must enlist forever: that is the shortest term on which Christ will take him.

V. 41, p. 259

GAMBLING

I do not hesitate to say that of all sins, there is none that more surely damns men than gambling, and worse than that it makes them the devil's helpers to damn others.

V. 45, p. 319

GIVING

Some people's religion is so spiritual that they cannot endure to hear of money, and they faint at the sound of a collection.

V. 30, p. 70

There is a thriftiness which we all ought to exercise; but to hoard up endless gold is a species of insanity.

V. 30, p. 190

GOOD WORKS

Luther was as sure that works could not save him as he was of his own existence.

V. 51, p. 57

We believe that men are saved by faith alone, but not by a faith which is alone: we are saved by faith without works, but not by a faith which is without works.

V. 21, p. 25, 26

If there be a faith (and there is) which leaves a man just what he was, and permits him to walk in sin, it is a faith of devils.

V. 27, p. 682

If Christ has finished the work for you which you could not do, now go and finish the work for him which you are privileged and permitted to do.

V. 40, p. 33

There is no reliance to be placed on anything you can do.
V. 61, p. 114

Men must give up trusting in their prayers, their tears, their repentance, their feelings and their church goings.
V. 61, p. 114

GOSPEL

If the gospel does not save you it will certainly be a curse to you.
V. 61, p. 117

A God condescending to bleed and die for his own enemies out of respect to justice, and moved by love; where in all heathen mythology is there anything like it?
V. 61, p. 283

If this is not true, it ought to be, for it is the grandest conception that ever flashed upon the human mind.
V. 61, p. 283

It seems to me so plainly a divine thing, so standing out of all conceptions of poetry, so distinctly rising out of all the realms of philosophy that it must be true.
V. 61, p. 283

No real faith was ever wrought in man by his own thoughts and imaginations; he much receive the gospel as a revelation from God, or he cannot receive it at all.
V. 25, p. 269

If a church of England minister preaches the gospel better than the Baptist minister does, do not go and hear the Baptist.
V. 61, p. 161

Here lies the power of the gospel, in that it gains the mastery over man's evil will, and without his consent changes his nature, and then fully gets his consent after his nature has been changed.
V. 45, p. 315

When ever you meet with teaching which is cloudy and complicated, you may generally conclude that it is not the gospel, for the truth of Christ is plain.
V. 13, p. 707

We are on the wrong ground when we begin to defend the gospel by reason.
V. 18, p. 716

GRACE

Make us the willing subjects of your grace or we shall become the unwilling slaves of your terror.
V. 2, p. 384

The more full a man is of grace the more he hungers for grace.
V. 27, p. 129

Oh what poor, faithless, treacherous, deceitful creatures we are: it is only grace that makes us anything worth having.
V. 39, p. 149

You who think you know him best, need constant supplies of his grace, else you would fall into the most sorrowful condition.
V. 46, p. 30

The more unfit you feel yourself to be, the more you are invited to come because your unfitness is your fitness for coming to Jesus.
V. 31, p. 682

When I confess myself to be weak, helpless, and ascribe all I have to grace, then I stand in the truth; but if I take the remotest praise to myself, I stand in a lie.
V. 22, p. 8

All men are negligent of their souls until grace gives them reason, then they leave their madness and act like rational beings.
M. & E., p. 613

Salvation by grace promotes good works far better than the teaching of salvation by works ever did, for those who hope to be saved by their works have generally very scanty works to be saved by.
V. 19, p. 682

True grace penetrates the very core of our nature, it changes the heart, subdues the will, renews the passions and makes us new creatures in Christ Jesus.
V. 11, p. 559

Though you deserve the depths of hell, yet up to the heights of heaven grace can lift you.
V. 59, p. 393

Oh for grace to fill out our poor shriveled lives till they arrive at a heavenly fullness.
V. 35, p. 228

Grace has spoiled you for the world, and there is no use attempting to get comfort out of it.
V. 35, p. 222

We feel surer as to the grace in a man's heart who groans after more grace, than we do of him who boasts—"I am rich and increased in good and have need of nothing."
V. 26, p. 596

The less worthy I am of his favors, the more sweetly will I sing of his grace.
V. 10, p. 720

Great sinners are glorious material for grace to work upon; and when you get them saved, they will shake the very gates of hell.
V. 51, p. 221

He has led us when we have been like Jonah, in the depths of the sea in very despair; and yet we are safe on dry ground.
V. 40, p. 40

Free grace is neither the child nor the father of human worthiness: if we get all the grace possible to get we can never be worthy of it.
V. 30, p. 353

To assume for a moment that we deserve anything of the Lord God, is so vain–glorious, so false, so unjust that we ought to loathe the very thought of it.

V. 30, p. 353

I do not object to books about self-made men, but I am afraid that self-made men have a tendency to worship him that made them.

V. 30, p. 354

No man could ever think that he deserved that the Son of God should die for him! if he does think so, he must be out of his mind.

V. 30, p. 355

"The very hairs of your head are all numbered" You are so precious that the least portion of you is precious.

V. 31, p. 51

Spiritual light shows us our emptiness, our poverty, our wretchedness but it reveals, in blessed contrast, his fullness, his riches, his freeness of grace.

V. 11, p. 644

Do I rejoice in that sovereign electing love which gave me to the Saviour for no reason whatever in me, but simply of his own free grace.

V. 44, p. 465

Christ will take the very castaways of the devil and use them for himself.

V. 44, p. 177

All those overwhelming debts, which would have sunk us to the lowest Hell, have been discharged; and they who believe in Christ may appear with boldness before the throne of God.

V. 40, p. 29

You shall measure your rising in grace by your sinking in humility.

V. 61, p. 236

God deals with sinners very honestly: he tells them what he wants and then deals with them very generously for he gives them what they need.
V. 61, p. 549

One day while reveling in the delights of being saved, and rejoicing in the doctrines of election, final perseverance and eternal glory, it came across my mind, "all this for you, for such a dead dog as you."
V. 60, p. 246

Think what grace there is in Christ Jesus our Lord; electing grace, calling grace, sanctifying grace, perfecting grace, grace upon grace that leads to glory.
V. 47, p. 380

Not all the tongues of men or angels can fully set forth the greatness of the grace of our redeemer.
V. 36, p. 96

That you should chose me, and call me, and pardon me, and save me, is a world of wonders at which my soul stands gratefully amazed.
V. 36, p. 472

What is grace but the morning twilight of glory.
V. 36, p. 74

He does not fling into the teeth of a sincere penitent any reproach concerning the past.
V. 28, p. 290

The dying thief—look what glory he has brought to Christ all through the centuries.
V. 28, p. 298

He knows that you are a thousand times worse than you think you are, still for all that he is ready to pardon.
V. 28, p. 299

This cultured age repudiates the doctrines of grace, which are the heart of evangelical teaching.
V. 32, p. 494

Free–will alone ruins men; but free-will guided by free grace is another matter.
V. 32, p. 503

A gospel for the cheerful would never have met my case; I wanted a gospel for the despairing.
V. 32, p. 358

Those whom free grace chooses, free grace cleanses.
V. 31, p. 442

He will forgive your anger if you repent of it, but if you tolerate it you are strangers to grace.
V. 15, p. 639

Publicans and harlots will enter into the kingdom of heaven before some of you, if you think you have a right to mercy.
V. 13, p. 305

Come as you are, sinful as you are, hardened as you are, careless as you think you are and have no good whatever, come to your God in Christ.
V. 14, p. 708

God's grace never increases; it is always infinite, always everlasting, always bottomless, always shoreless.
V. 46, p. 530

The same grace that can preserve a child of God from falling into sin can bring a sinner out of sin.
V. 39, p. 93

We may look upon every past act of grace as being a token and guarantee of future grace.
V. 12, p. 657

O for grace to get our temper under our foot and keep it there, for anger is temporary insanity.
V. 12, p. 355

I stand here to preach limitless love, boundless grace, to the vilest of the vile, to those who have nothing in them, that could deserve consideration from God.
V. 41, p. 5

GREAT MEN OF GOD
᠙

I think sometimes, that I would not mind changing places with George Müller for time and for eternity but I do not know anybody else of whom I would say as much as that.
V. 49, p. 238

The first ministers of Christ were a band of fishermen and countrymen, so the grandest era in the world's history was ushered in by nobodies.
V. 26, p. 676

Paul's life was divided into two periods,—first he was the persecutor, and then he was persecuted.
V. 51, p. 394

Godly Whitefield, when smitten with a dangerous illness, rose again to renew his seraphic activities after his death had become a matter of daily expectation.
V. 55, p. 341

HEALING
᠙

When medicine heals us, it is because God makes it the means of healing.
V. 45, p. 450

Time is a wonderful healer, hearts that seem as if they must break when first the trial comes, at last grow quite used to it.
V. 46, p. 243

HEAVEN
᠙

The meanest soul in heaven knows more of God than the greatest saint on earth.
V. 3, p. 315

Let us walk in unbroken fellowship with him—so we shall get two heavens, a little heaven below and a boundless heaven above when our turn shall come to go home.
V. 19, p. 576

Saints who are among the brightest in heaven, have yet in their day sat weeping at the gates of despair.
V. 19, p. 688

There cannot be heaven without Christ, he is the sum total of bliss; the fountain from which heaven flows, the element of which heaven is composed.
V.19, p. 571

Have you not conceived great ideas of what the Lord will make out of you when you shall be washed, and cleansed, and delivered from sin, and carried away to serve him in Heaven.
V. 21, p. 665

When you and I enter heaven, it will not be going from bad to good but from good to better.
V. 21, p. 665

You must learn the music here, or you will never sing in the choirs of heaven.
V. 27, p. 191

It will be no small heaven for God himself to appreciate our poor lives.
V. 31, p. 669

If there were nothing else to expect in Heaven but that we should know Christ better and love him more, that is all the heaven that any of us should desire.
V. 1, p. 331 Autobiography

There would not be one hundredth part so much difference between earth and heaven if we did not live so far below our privileges.
V. 36, p. 73

The richest saint in glory has no greater possession than his God.
V. 36, p. 75

If it were possible, when we get to heaven, one of the things we should do would be to sit down and laugh at our fears.
V. 34, p. 670

Christ has gone to prepare your place and it would be wrong for you to have no desire for it.
V. 24, p. 131

To clutch the pleasure of an hour, all earth–stained as they are, shall we renounce the ecstasies of eternity.
V. 25, p. 189

God is making, by his grace, beings who will stand next to his throne, but will remain reverently loyal forever.
V. 25, p. 189

I thought the saints would be perfect, but I never imagined such a transfiguration of excessive glory would be upon each of them.
V. 25, p. 318

Deliverance from sin will be an escape from all sorrow, and the obtaining of perfect holiness will be the climax of delight.
V. 14, p. 653

"Thy will be done on earth as it is in heaven," teaches us that the angels do the will of God perfectly, cheerfully, instantly with the highest possible alacrity.
V. 14, p. 652

The pains of this mortal life will seem to be a mere pin–prick to us when we get into the joys never ending and overflowing.
V. 13, p. 434

Although we have to struggle through this one brief hour of toil and conflict, an hour with God in glory will make up for it all.
V. 13, p. 434

In heaven, mysteries which perplex us now shall be simplicities then.
V. 20, p. 321

HELL
~

There are many in hell who once were almost saved, but who are now altogether dammed.
V. 252, p. 258

In proportion to the light against which you have shut your eyes will be your horror when that light shall blind you into eternal darkness.
V. 26, p. 72

They shall remember that they were called, but would not come; that they were wooed, but hardened their necks and chose their own delusions.
V. 60, p. 189

It is hell to lose heaven, it is infinite misery to miss infinite felicity.
V. 25, p. 186

Despising God by neglecting Him or forgetting Him is a grievous kind of despising Him that will bring men to eternal ruin.
V. 55, p. 357

All the pangs, and rocks, and abandonment from which men suffer here are nothing to be compared with the woes and mental anguish of the world to come.
V. 15, p. 707

Think lightly of hell and you will think lightly of the cross.
V. 12, p. 174

Think little of the suffering of lost souls and you will soon think little of the Savior who delivers you from them.
V. 12, p. 174

Scripture does not speak of the fires of hell as chastening and purifying, but as punishment for deeds done in the body.
V. 12, p. 177

If the wooings of Christ's wounds cannot make you love him, do you think the flames of hell will?
V. 12, p. 177

There cannot be a more terrible hell for a man than to be in the grasp of his memory and of his conscience in the last great day.
V. 44, p. 18

HOLINESS

Souls that sigh for holiness are not condemned to eternal death, for their sighing proves that they are in Christ Jesus.
V. 32, p. 470

We do not expect sinless perfection this side of the grave, but we do expect perfection in desire, perfection of intention, perfection in heart aspiration.
V. 57, p. 406

Of all the griefs the church ever feels, the keenest is when those who once stood in her midst dishonor the name of Christ by unholy living.
V. 43, p. 427

There can be no such thing as perfect happiness till there is perfect holiness.
V. 24, p. 642

Sin will grow without sowing but holiness needs cultivation.
V. 16, p. 340

The holier a man becomes, the more he mourns the unholiness which remains in him.
V. 26, p. 635

No Christian can have a sacred ambition for holiness which the Lord is not prepared to fulfill.
V. 23, p. 282

True godliness is such a thing as no saint dares to trifle with.
V. 44, p. 296

It is not for us to live as others live, who walk in the vanity of their minds: we are not to seek the world's pleasures or defile ourselves with its folly.
V. 26, p. 636

Your real character no man can injure but yourself; and if you are enabled to keep your garments clean, all else is not worth a thought.
V. 37, p. 38

I do not ask you if you are perfect, but I do ask whether you follow the Perfect One.
V. 51, p. 57-58

Brethren, if I find Christ contradicting everything that I ever thought, I would, without regret, fling every thought in my mind to the winds.
V. 41, p. 32

Oh, that the Lord would cause you to see sin in its true colours, and holiness in its own splendour.
V. 30, p. 199

Christ's righteousness is set to our account, so that faith is reckoned unto us for righteousness.
V. 29, p. 128

Did I hear one remark, "I cannot see this way of righteousness"? I answer, No, and you never will until the Spirit of God convinces you of it.
V. 29, p. 128

All those who trust in Christ are for his sake regarded as righteousness before God.
V. 29, p. 128

He that has a clean heart will necessarily have clean hands.
V. 31, p. 154

Beware, I pray you, of any pretense to a holiness arising out of yourselves, and maintained by the energy of your own unaided wills.
V. 25, p. 315

We have not experienced what perfection is, and therefore we can hardly conceive it; our thoughts themselves are too sinful for us to get a full idea of what absolute perfection must be.
V. 25, p. 319

Let us prove the sincerity of our confidence in Christ by the holiness of our lives.
V. 16, p. 191

God knows and approves each true believer, and each true believer proves his knowledge of God and his delight in him by departing from evil.
V. 31, p. 440

Forordination to holiness is indissolubly joined to forordination to happiness.
V. 31, p. 153

No furnace ever purifies our hearts like the love of Jesus, which burns like coals of juniper.
V. 33, p. 514

Full assurance cannot exist with unholiness.
V. 44, p. 29

A pure theology and a loose morality will never blend.
V. 24, p. 627

A disciple of the Lord Jesus Christ indulging in covetousness is a self–evident contradiction.
V. 24, p. 629

HOLY SPIRIT

There is not a grain of holiness beneath the sky but what is the operation of the Holy Spirit.
V. 23, p. 20

With Jesus himself slain as an atonement, Jesus exalted as a prince and a saviour at the right hand of God, and with the divine Spirit abiding with us forever, what is there impossible to the church of God?

V. 32, p. 94

We never go an inch toward heaven in any other power than that of the Holy Spirit.

V. 35, p. 226

The more he fills us with his Spirit, the more will our own spirit sink within us in utter amazement that he should ever make use of such broken vessels as we are!

V. 41, p. 303

Let us feel that we are so many pipes connected to one fountain; and therefore as all the good we do comes from one source, let us give all the honour and glory of it to the Spirit of God from whom it comes.

V. 47, p. 406

The weakness of faith is ours, but the strength of faith comes from the Holy Spirit.

V. 59, p. 78–79

You and I had not life enough to know our death until the Holy Spirit visited us, we had not light enough to perceive that we were in darkness, nor sense enough to feel our misery.

V. 23, p. 15

There is no spiritual good in all the world of which He is not the author and sustainer, and heaven itself will owe the perfect character of its redeemed inhabitants to his work.

M. & E., p. 95

If an angel should fly from heaven and inform the saint personally of the Saviour's love to him, the evidence would not be one whit more satisfactory than that which is borne in the heart by the Holy Spirit.

M. & E., p. 710

The wind, though we have no control over it, has a law of its own, and the Holy Spirit is a law unto himself; he does as he wills, but he wills to do evermore that which is for the best.
V. 23, p. 305

If the people of God meet together and besiege the throne of grace with cries and tears, the spiritual barometer indicates that the blessed wind is rising.
V. 23, p. 305

There are secrets which nature does not reveal, and the work of the Spirit is even more a secret, and assuredly no man can explain it to his fellow or to himself.
V. 23, p. 309

The Holy Spirit, when you are full of him, makes you quiet with a deep, unutterable peace.
V. 35, p. 584

I wish that some Christian people were filled with the Spirit, if there were no other effect produced upon them but that of peace, self–possession, restfulness and freedom from passion.
V. 35, p. 58

The Spirit of God works submissiveness of mind: instead of wanting to be first, the truly spiritual man will be satisfied to be last, if he can thus glorify God.
V. 35, p. 585

I have prayed that when the spirit which grows out of our association with each other declines we may be sustained by the Spirit who unites us all to the Lord Jesus.
V. 25, p. 282

There were seven thousand people whose knees had never been bent to Baal; for the still small voice had been doing for Israel what Elijah could not do.
V. 55, p. 557–558

Teachers may put holy thoughts into our heads but they cannot change our hearts.
V. 27, p. 574

A single word, spoken in the strength of God, will effect far more than ten thousand words uttered in the power of mere reasoning, or eloquence, or even earnestness.
V. 40, p. 76

If you think that you have experienced the work of the Holy Spirit in your heart, and yet it does not draw you to Christ, you have made a mistake.
V. 40, p. 535

The miseries which the Holy Spirit works are always the prelude to happiness.
V. 17, p. 382

Better to be broken in pieces by the Spirit of God, than to be made whole by the flesh.
V. 17, p. 382

All the arguments in the world do not convince the human heart unless the Spirit of all grace shall come and change the nature.
V. 61, p. 284

How the Holy Spirit directly operates on the soul we do not know; it is one of the great mysteries of grace.
V. 28, p. 609

If I worship the Father and the Son, but forget or neglect to adore the Holy Spirit, I worship less than God.
V. 28, p. 301

We enjoy less of his power and see less of his working in the world because the church of God has not been sufficiently mindful of him.
V. 28, p. 301

The Holy Spirit was with the Apostles in the days when Jesus was with them; but he was not in them in the sense in which he filled them at and after the Day of Pentecost.
V. 28, p. 304

The descending Spirit is the noblest testimony among men to the glory of the ascending redeemer.
V. 28, p. 305

The Holy Spirit uses the hearing of the Word of God for the conviction, conversion, consolation and sanctification of men.
V. 28, p. 306

The presence of Jesus Christ was of inestimable value to his disciples, and yet it was not such an advantage as the indwelling of the Holy Spirit.
V. 28, p. 306

The Holy Spirit is our strength, our glory, the abiding witness that our great leader is Lord and God.
V. 18, p. 716

What a marvel that Deity should be said to grieve over the faults of beings so utterly insignificant as we are.
V. 13, p. 121

You can do nothing without the Holy Spirit; therefore do nothing that would cause him to depart from you.
V. 38, p. 115

Even the sacrifice of Christ on the cross does not avail for you until the Holy Spirit takes of the things of Christ and reveals them unto you.
V. 58, p. 183

He has gone to heaven to prepare a place for me and he has sent his Spirit down to earth to prepare me for the place.
V. 48, p. 333

HOPE

A world without God is a world without fear, without law, without order, without hope.
V. 35, p. 663

It is good for you to remember what you used to be, for then you will have hope for other people.
V. 51, p. 395

There is something within us that tells us we are immortal, or there is at any rate, something that makes us hope we are, and shrink with loathing from the idea of being annihilated.
V. 60, p. 176

The existence of an immortal soul in man is taken for granted in scripture.
V. 32, p. 13

We carry a bag of spending money in our hands, but the bulk of our wealth is deposited in the Bank of Hope.
V. 25, p. 184

HUMAN WEAKNESS

The weaker I am the more room there is for God to get the glory.
V. 60, p. 248

The doorstep of wisdom is a consciousness of ignorance, and the gateway of perfection is a deep sense of imperfection.
V. 45, p. 263

Paul was never so nearly perfect as when he cried, "O wretched man that I am! who shall deliver me from this body of death?"
V. 45, p. 263

Do not deny the strong man his meat, but let him have as much as he likes of it; as for yourself, if you are a babe in grace, keep to your milk diet.
V. 45, p. 264

Man is like to vanity, and no more to be relied upon than the mist of the morning.
V. 36, p. 308

The most unworthy people are generally those who boast of their worthiness.
V. 36, p. 469

No man can have too low an opinion of his own power; because he has no power whatever.
V. 36, p. 615

If we have strong faith we shall glory in our powerlessness, because the power of Christ does rest upon us.
V. 36, p. 615

We may become just a little too spiritual, so spiritual as to spirit away the very spirit of Christianity.
V. 24, p. 374

Have you had little else than defeat? this is the way to success: you will pave the road with the rough flints of your failure.
V. 24, p. 503

Our spirits cannot comprehend the infinite, but we believe in God, and are sure that he orders all things aright.
V. 24, p. 714

Only as you become consciously weak would you become actually strong.
V. 24, p. 123

The Lord must first enlighten the eyes of our understanding or else, however clearly the truth may be stated, we shall never be able to understand it.
V. 25, p. 181

He who sees most needs to have his eyes enlightened to see more, for little as yet of the glory of God have any of us beheld.
V. 25, p. 182

Man is a strange mixture; he is next akin to Deity and yet he is brother to the worm.
V. 25, p. 189

He who is his own guide is guided by a fool.
V. 50, p. 353

He that trusts in his own understanding proves that he has no understanding.
V. 50, p. 353

Distrust yourself, dear friend, for you accurately gauge your own judgment when you do that.
V. 50, p. 354

How can one talk about directing his own steps when he is absolutely dependent upon the grace of God for every step he takes.
V. 50, p. 356

When you feel certain that you cannot go wrong, you certainly will go wrong unless you ask counsel of God.
V. 50, p. 355

Many want to know the ninth of Romans before they read the third of John; they are all for understanding great mysteries before they understand that primary simplicity, "believe and live."
V. 16, p. 166

Disclosures of our weakness and sinfulness are often made to us at the very time when God is honoring us the most.
V. 13, p. 242

Your inability does not prevent the working of his power; your unworthiness cannot put fetters to his bounty or limits to his grace.
V. 14, p. 148

Your sense of unworthiness should lead you to a simple faith in Jesus.
V. 14, p. 139

He has much pity for our weakness, and I wish that some of his servants had more of the same spirit.
V. 42, p. 134

A headlong zeal even for Christ may leap into a ditch.
V. 38, p. 114

A man of no desire gets what he longs for; and that is nothing at all.
V. 38, p. 117

If a man will not do anything until he has solved every difficulty, we had better dig his grave.

V. 38, p. 119

The weakest and meanest of God's people are as necessary as
the noblest and most beautiful.

V. 38, p. 87

The fault with a great many Christians is that they have only
just light enough to see things as in a mist.

V. 39, p. 51

If somebody were to assert that I am not here, and that I am
not speaking, I have no doubt that with proper pay, a lawyer
could be found to prove it.

V. 39, p. 186

Men weep at a theater, and weep far more than they do in
many places of worship; therefore, merely weeping under a
sermon is no sign of having profited therefrom.

V. 11, p. 496

The most superstitious people in the world are those who are
most profane.

V. 11, p. 342

We may be indulging an unchristian, intolerant spirit in our
zeal against intolerance.

V. 41, p. 314

We may even deceive ourselves into the belief that we are
honoring our Lord when we are, all the while, bringing disgrace upon his name.

V. 41, p. 314

It is to the honour of our Lord Jesus Christ that his cause and
his character survive all the follies and sins of his people.

V. 41, p. 314

We may have all the decencies of morality, and all the propri-
eties of Christian conduct, and yet we may be all the while
"departing from the living God."

V. 44, p. 28

The moment we begin to trust in man and make flesh our arm we have to that extent forgotten God.
V. 44, p. 28

They who can trifle with heavenly things are not true believers in the Lord Jesus Christ.
V. 44, p. 29

The very anxiety which arises through your difficulty unfits you to meet that difficulty.
V. 50, p. 87

If I could comprehend the whole of revelation I could scarcely believe it to be divine.
V. 12, p. 232

People want "clever" men to preach the gospel: I question whether the devil himself has ever wrought so much mischief in the church of God as clever men have done.
V. 42, p. 236

There is only a certain amount of thought and energy in a man; and if the world gets it, Christ cannot have it.
V. 34, p. 474

We may follow the man as far as the man follows Christ, but not an inch farther.
V. 35, p. 51

To be associated with some who are not true seems inevitable in this life, however carefully we choose our company.
V. 35, p. 311

Oh, my brethren, it is vain and idle for us to think that any good can come of human speech or human song or worship apart from God himself being there.
V. 25, p. 285

There must be supernatural power put forth or men will never turn from darkness to light.
V. 25, p. 285

It often happens in the commencement of religious movements that men are weak and few and feeble and despised, but they trust in God, and so they grow strong, but their strength becomes their overthrow.
V. 25, p. 282

Man's strength is more in God's way than man's weakness.
V. 10, p. 435

I am old enough to be weary with observing the imperfections of my brothers and sisters in Christ, and I prefer to spy out their excellencies, and take delight in them.
V. 55, p. 616

I find it better to commend my brethren than to censure them and discourage them by the censure.
V. 55, p. 616

We can find a thousand flaws in our best works, and when we lie dying, we shall still have to lament our shortcomings and excesses.
V. 40, p. 26

We who are getting into years, and have a long experience, are just the kind of stone that the devil likes to carve into monuments of our own folly.
V. 40, p. 44

I hope we agree with God as to our own unworthiness and helplessness, so that we look to him alone.
V. 10, p. 618

I find it better to think well of God's people than to think ill of them.
V. 55, p. 616

HUMILITY

Let us humble ourselves and entreat the heavenly dew to rest upon us, the sacred oil to anoint us and the celestial flame to burn within us.
Morn. and Eve., p. 87

The engrafted soul–saving word is not received except with meekness.
Morn. and Eve., p. 431

That is not true faith but spurious, which is not humble; and that is not genuine humility which is not confident in God.
V. 13, p. 248

We are all of us remarkably good–tempered when we have our own way; but the true meekness, which is a work of grace, will endure the test of enmity, cruelty and wrong, even as Christ did upon the cross.
V. 53, p. 547

The humbler a man lies, the more comfort he will always have, because he will be more fitted to receive it.
Morn. and Eve., p. 86

When I confess myself to be weak, helpless, and ascribe all I have to grace, then I stand in the truth; but if I take even the remotest praise to myself, I stand in a lie.
V. 22, p. 8

It is well to be weak in self and better still to be nothing.
V. 23, p. 17

Your humblings are nothing but another form of pride unless your soul has a reverent and deep respect for the Lord.
V. 13, p. 244

We are never safer, never healthier, never in a better position than when we are right flat down on the ground before the cross.
V. 15, p. 24

Humble walking with God is so difficult to come by that thousands sit down content with that which looks like it, but is by no means the same thing.

V. 26, p. 515

True humility does not continually talk about "dust and ashes," and prate about its infirmities, but it feels all that which others say, for it possesses an inwrought feeling of its own nothingness.

V. 2, p. 351

Humility is a thing which must be genuine; the imitation of it is the nearest thing in the world to pride.

V. 2, p. 351

There is nothing about ourselves worth thinking of apart from Christ; and it will be well to dismiss the thought.

V. 24, p. 84

Did you ever feel the bliss of dying to self? As you near the vanishing point of self the glory of the Lord downs on you with immeasurable splendor.

V. 35, p. 119

Many a boy at school does not learn any thing for he is conceited: he knows nothing and teaches himself.

V. 35, p. 51

It is God's way to smite the strong with weakness, and to bless the weak with strength.

V. 26, p. 45

Self–humiliation is the native spirit of the true–born child of God.

V. 13, p. 647

We are fit for Christ's service so long as we feel that as yet we have done nothing, and are merely at the beginning of our proposed service.

V. 25, p. 283

An omnipotent hand created us out of nothing and the like omnipotence is needed to bring us to feel that we are nothing.

V. 55, p. 378

An ungodly world may consider the poor in spirit to be contemptible, but God writes them down among his peers and princes.
V. 55, p. 382

When you have done with self, then Christ will be all–in–all to you.
V. 51, p. 188

A humble man mourns over his pride daily; it is only a proud man who has any humility to boast of.
V. 18, p. 371

Everywhere before salvation there comes the humbling of the creature, the overthrow of human hope.
V. 17, p. 378

It would be better to believe that, if you are earnest, there are others who are still more earnest.
V. 47, p. 74

We must come as humble petitioners, and not as those who proudly fancy that they have a claim upon the grace of God.
V. 36, p. 472

If you are weighed down with a sense of your own unworthiness, you will weather any gale that may come upon you.
V. 50, p. 65

When the grace of God works in us, we are made to feel that the very lowest and meanest place is a better position than we have any right to take.
V. 50, p. 91

A broken heart alone becomes a believing heart, and an assured heart must first be a humble heart.
V. 16, p. 346

You know not how many temporal griefs would vanish away like smoke before the wind if your heart was humbler before the Most High.
V. 16, p. 153

The state of humility is much more blessed than the mere act of humiliation, and should be the condition of every Christian at all times.
V. 13, p. 245

We who sprang from nothing, and must go back to nothing, shall we boast about ourselves?
V. 13, p. 246

That is not true faith but spurious which is not humble; and that is not genuine humility which is not confident in God.
V. 13, p. 48

True humility is forming a just estimate of oneself to bring oneself down where one ought to be.
V. 13, p. 248

Many times in the history of Israel when they were given over to their enemies, their humbling themselves at once drove away the invaders and set them free of the scourge!
V. 13, p. 248

This basest of all men, this wicked Ahab, yet obtained a blessing from God when he humbled himself.
V. 13, p. 249

Make a vacuum by humility and God will fill that vacuum by his love.
V. 13, p. 249

Faith itself cannot be strong where humility is weak.
V. 13, p. 250

There is nothing that has such power over ungodly men as meekness of spirit, patience of character and continual conquest over an evil temper.
V. 38, p. 17

We are robbed of the meaning of that word, "the joy of the Lord is your strength" unless we believe simply like children.
V. 38, p. 93

Do you want to have sinners broken down under a sense of sin? then you must be broken down yourself.
V. 38, p. 116

Humble yourselves in wonder that God should permit your name to stand on the roll of his elect at all.
V. 41, p. 303

God puts the beauty of his own brightness upon meek men; not upon great men, nor upon those who profess to be great.
V. 43, p. 126

He who is humble still laments his pride, and thus shows his humility better than in any other way.
V. 44, p. 21

Let the man be earnest, but first let him be humble.
V. 44, p. 115

The more grace we have, the less we shall think of ourselves, for grace, like light, reveals our impurity.
M. & E., p. 297

HUMOR

Humour is a faculty of nature, and ought to be consecrated and used for the cause of Christ.
V. 20, p. 165

Sometimes when I have used a humorous thing in preaching I have not asked you to excuse me, for if God has given me humour I mean to use it in his cause.
V. 20, p. 165

The true Christian can laugh as every honest man can, but he is not a constant giggler and hunter after childish merriment, as many are.
V. 55, p. 614

HYPOCRISY
ℛ

If I must perish, I would rather perish as an openly–avowed sinner than as a hypocrite.
V. 10, p. 672

High professors take care, you may go to the gates of heaven by profession; but there is a back door to hell.
V. 10, p. 672

The bended knee is nothing, the prostrate heart is everything.
V. 20, p. 327

Men have gone forth making use of the name of Jesus and God has honoured the name, though he has not accepted the men who used it.
V. 22, p. 604

Good seed will grow even though it is scattered by a leprous hand.
V. 22, p. 604

No one can do so much damage to the church of God as the man who is within its walls, but not within its life.
V. 35, p. 310

I never met a hypocrite who thought himself to be one.
V. 35, p. 311

If there is a special thunderbolt anywhere, it is these unctuous hypocrites who whine about love to Christ, and bow down at the shrine of mammon.
V. 10, p. 106

Some turn to hypocrisy, thinking that to pretend to be holy will be as good as being so.
V. 14, p. 671

Whenever a man is about to stab religion, he usually professes very great reverence for it.
M. & E., p. 170

To kneel down and say, "Lord have mercy upon us miserable sinners," and then get up and feel yourself a very decent sort, worthy of commendation, is to mock Almighty God.
V. 37, p. 225

If we preach against hypocrisy, hypocrites will say, "Admirable," "Admirable!" if we preach against secret sin, secret sinners will say, "An excellent discourse."
V. 11, p. 163–164

A thousand Christians can scarcely do such honour to their master as one hypocrite can do to dishonour him.
v.10, p. 96

A very numerous class have opinion but not faith, we are grossly mistaken if we think orthodoxy of creed will save us.
V. 10, p. 99

I am sick of those cries of "the truth," "the truth" from men of rotten lives and unholy tempers.
V. 10, p. 99

There is an orthodox as well as a heterodox road to hell, and the devil knows how to handle Calvinists as well as Armenians.
V. 10, p. 99

If you pray without sincerity the Lord will be tired of your mockery of prayer.
V. 44, p. 433

It is only natural that there should be hypocrites; there never was a good thing in the world but what people did make a sham of it.
V. 61, p. 284

There are some who have no intention to be hypocrites, but still all the grace they have is but sham grace.
V. 61, p. 543

Delude not yourself with the thought that you have holy desires unless you truly have them.
V. 61, p. 545

My heart is wounded with the sight of some who come into God's house and undertake God's service and yet during the week they are unjust, oppressive, graceless and greedy.
V. 31, p. 436

Whatever sin we may fall into, God save us from hypocrisy, and make us honest and straight forward in all things.
V. 41, p. 93

Oh brethren and sisters, be before men what you are before God! seem to be what you really are.
V. 41, p. 303

We cannot help observing that there are unbelievers who bear the name of Christian.
V. 44, p. 30

IMPATIENCE

We shall not grow weary of waiting upon God if we remember how long and how graciously He waited for us.
M. & E., p. 381

Unanswered petitions are not unheard; God keeps a file of our prayers, they are treasured in the King's archives.
V. 13, p. 74

Will not the Lord's time be better than your time?
V. 13, p. 74

"Stand still"—keep the posture of a man ready for action, expecting further orders, while cheerfully and patiently awaiting the directing voice.
M. & E., p. 412

Beware of having so much to do that you really do nothing at all because you do not wait upon God to do it aright.
V. 49, p. 404

By his wisdom he so orders His delays, that they prove to be far better than our hurries.
V. 14, p. 84

INCARNATION
℀

He willingly stooped to the lowest position to save the lowest of men.
V. 19, p. 198

The Lord Jesus has taken manhood into union with the divine nature, and now between God and man there exists a special and unparalleled relationship, the like of which the universe cannot present.
V. 21, p. 67

The humanity of Christ has a charm about it which the quietly sorrowful alone discover.
V. 23, p. 693

I have know what it is to gaze upon the incarnation with calm repose of heart when my brain has seemed to be on fire with anguish.
V. 23, p. 693

The coming of God in human flesh is the lone star of the world's night.
V. 36, p. 493

It is a miracle of miracles that the Infinite should become an infant.
V. 36, p. 495

Why has he taken our nature in its sorrow, but that we may be partakers of the divine nature in righteousness and holiness?
V. 36, p. 496

Oh that the people who walk in darkness may see in the incarnate God a great light, and perceive in him the prophesy and assurance of all good things!
V. 36, p. 496

If any man should attempt to explain or even define the union of the divine and human in the Lord Jesus, he would soon prove his folly.
V. 13, p. 699

If the son of God be man, then he understands me and will
have a fellow feeling for me.
V. 18, p. 714

JOY

In the absence of all other joys, the joy of the Lord can fill the
soul to the brim.
V. 13, p. 113

The golden oil that feeds the lamp of the Christian's joy is not
drawn from the wells of the earth.
V. 54, p. 38

Sit down now, beloved, and let your soul triumph to the last
degree of joy in this—your name is written in heaven.
V. 22, p. 609

Many a child of God goes fretting and worrying when he
ought to be singing and rejoicing, and would do so if he
knew what God had provided for him.
V. 34, p. 287

I think the happiest days the church of Christ ever had have
been her days of persecution.
V. 41, p. 64

He that made the world out of nothing can certainly restore
the joy you have lost.
V. 53, p. 176

I cannot bear to see religion served up with vinegar; it ought
to be sweet in itself—so sweet that if you poured a cask of
vinegar on it you would not make it sour.
V. 46, p. 427

Perfection of holiness must mean perfection of happiness, the
two things must go together, sin and sorrow cannot be
divorced, and holiness and happiness cannot be separated.
V. 49, p. 19

Nothing beneath the skies and nothing above the skies, can make any man happy apart form God, search as you will.
V. 22, p. 419

Is it not strange that Christian men should be in a position which angels might envy and yet they fail to realize their blest estate.
V. 23, p. 341

Here you are, accepted in the Beloved, and conscious of being adopted into the family of heaven, and for all that your joy is at a low ebb.
V. 23, p. 341

Beloved if we are not as happy as the days are long in these summer months, it is entirely our own fault, for there is plenty of reason for being so.
V. 23, p. 341

In other things men are always sharp enough to look after what they call "number one" but when it comes to the purest happiness that can be had, they are so foolish as to let everything else attract them more than the Lord Jesus.
V. 24, p. 84

Many people have religion enough to make them wretched if they had seven times as much, they would be joyful.
V. 35, p. 612

Let us rejoice when conversion is wrought by instruments that cannot take the glory for it.
V. 26, p. 679

It is one of the joys of the great Father's heart to make his children glad.
V. 26, p. 599

Be assured, my dear friend, it is no joy to God to see you with that dreary countenance.
V. 26, p. 299

The man who has a hope of the next world goes about his work strong, for the joy of the Lord is our strength.
V. 10, p. 190

Our hope in Christ for the future is the mainstream of our joy.
V. 10, p. 189

My brother, sometimes your spirit sinks within you; but do you not count yourself to be, even at your worst, happier than the worldling at his best?
V. 27, p. 75

You may not at this moment be conscious of joy: trees are not always bearing fruit, and yet their substance is in them when they loose their leaves.
V. 27, p. 77

Joy comes not from what we have but what we are.
V. 27, p. 77

O this is wondrous grace, this joy which can live side be side with conflict of the worst kind.
V. 27, p. 78

If men could guess what delicious droughts are held within the chalice of divine communion they would be ready to wade through hell itself to drink from it.
V. 27, p. 78

The joy of my heart when I think of the doctrine of election is quite inexpressible.
V. 27, p. 79

Cheerfulness we are to cultivate, but we must beware lest levity become a cankerworm to our graces.
V. 14, p. 94

If any of you have lost the joy of the Lord, I pray you do not think it a small loss.
V. 60, p. 231

Christian, can you believe yourself "loved with an everlasting love," and not rejoice?
V. 60, p. 232

Our joy ends where love of the world begins.
V. 60, p. 234

Fellowship with Christ is the summum bonum; it fills up the measure of joy.
V. 60, p. 235

Every precept in the Word of God is intended to further the Christian's happiness.
V. 60, p. 235

Holy activity is the mother of holy joy.
V. 60, p. 236

No man is so happy but he would be happier still if he had true religion.
V. 47, p. 613

If Jesus spoke the truth, the believer has everlasting life; happiness becomes a duty and peace a matter of obligation.
V. 28, p. 70

As oil to the wheels of a machine, so is cheerfulness to a man's conversation.
V. 50, p. 64

I fully believe that there was never on the face of the earth a man who knew so profound and true a gladness as our blessed Lord.
V. 22, p. 27

His deep joy was concealed by his many griefs.
V. 22, p. 28

If you are severely afflicted it will need all your joyfulness to keep you from sinking.
V. 22, p. 28

Christ was a man of sorrows, but he was not a preacher of sorrows.
V. 22, p. 28

He was both the greatest rejoicer and the greatest mourner that ever lived.
V. 22, p. 28

The joy of our Lord Jesus Christ now that he knows his beloved are securely his, and no longer slaves to sin, and heirs of wrath, is too great to be measured.
V. 22, p. 29

The Saviour looks upon the redeemed with an unspeakable delight.
V. 22, p. 30

In Christ we come into the condition in which it is safe for us to be glad and possible for joy to dwell in us.
V. 22, p. 32

Ignorance means sorrow, but the light of the knowledge of God in the face of Jesus Christ means joy.
V. 22, p. 34

Sometimes when we realize our oneness with Christ, we can hardly think that we should be happier in heaven.
V. 38, p. 95

Our greatest joys swim on the crest of huge billows of trouble.
V. 35, p. 334

There is no sweeter, more thrilling delight to be known this side of heaven than that of having Christ's joy fulfilled in us that our joy may be full.
V. 11, p. 117

If your religion does not make you rejoice, it is not worth much.
V. 41, p. 259

"Rejoice in the Lord always;" that is, when you cannot rejoice in anything or anyone but God.
V. 41, p. 138

He who has never felt the burden of sin will, I think, never know the joy of faith.
V. 43, p. 518

There is more joy in the sufferings of Christ, to those whose hearts are broken, than there is in his birth, or his resurrection or anything else about the Savior.
V. 44, p. 272

JUDGMENT

All that nature spins, time will unravel, to the eternal confusion of all who are clothed therein.
M. & E., p. 288

Judas! you hanged yourself to escape the judgment of your conscience, but by no means can you escape the judgment of God!
V. 27, p. 312

No stray thought of yours, no imagination, no trifle which you have quite forgotten has escaped your heavenly father's notice.
V. 22, p. 93

Judgment must begin in the House of God; the Lord may let the wicked remain in this world for many a day unpunished, but if you come near to him he will be sanctified in you or upon you.
V. 31, p. 443

Rejecters of great mercy must expect great wrath.
V. 23, p. 658

If you have to judge of a man's state, and know but little of it, always judge it favorably.
V. 26, p. 68

We expect to stand before the judgment seat in the midst of a great assembly, but still to be judged as if no other person were there.
V. 13, p. 641

I know of no mercy under heaven for any man who, knowing of the atoning sacrifice, willfully puts it away.
V. 26, p. 633

It will go hard with those who leap into Hell-fire over a father's prayers and a mother's entreaties.
V. 27, p. 530

Nothing could be more cruel than to allow men to sin without being punished for it.
V. 41, p. 31

Saints are judged now by a fatherly discipline, that they may not be judged hereafter by a judicial condemnation.
V. 30, p. 431

He that perverts truth shall soon be incapable of knowing the true from the false.
V. 31, p. 321

God would not, even for mercy's sake, issue an unjust pardon to the souls he loved.
V. 31, p. 318

Think not lightly of the doom of the lost, lest you think lightly of sin and lightly of Christ.
V. 60, p. 119

The curse which God pronounced on the serpent is pronounced on the whole of his seed, and everything that is impure, untruthful and unholy lies under the ban of God.
V. 36, p. 522

If by means of doing evil we should rise to wealth, honour and ease, we should find all our gains a burning curse.
V. 36, p. 522

He who does not believe that God will punish sin, will not believe that God will pardon it.
V. 28, p. 20

You can be justified through him by whom you shall be judged at the last great day.
V. 32, p. 501

Many a man's life has come to an end when he wished it to be continued and he has missed that which he has striven for because of an offense against the Lord committed in his earlier years.
V. 33, p. 318

Nadab and Abihu died before the Lord because they offered strange fire, while many another man lived on in the blackest iniquities.
V. 31, p. 443

See how he dealt with Ananias and Sapphira within the church, while many a liar outside of it grows gray in falsehood.
V. 31, p. 443

Rest assured your calling and your position will be no excuse for your sin.
V. 14, p. 145

JUSTIFICATION

When the believer has to cry out in the agony of his spirit because of the vehemence of temptation, he may still lay his hand upon the Word of God and say, "there is no condemnation to me for I am in Christ Jesus."
Vol. 32, p. 469

The prisoner has pleaded guilty to the capital charge, and has borne the utmost penalty of the law by his substitute, which penalty God himself has accepted.
V. 25, p. 66

God the Father would never have given up his only–begotten Son to die for human guilt, if there had been any other way of saving lost sinners.
V. 50, p. 496

When Christ bore the sins of his people the justice of God was more honored than it would have been if all the elect had been sent to hell forever.
V. 50, p. 501

If the righteousness of Christ girds you, even the eye of God cannot see a spot in you.
V. 11, p. 115

KINDNESS

Among religious persons kindness toward man should be as manifest as piety toward God.
V. 24, p. 373

If there be two ways of understanding a sentence, my brother, and one is better than the other, always read it in the kindest way, if you can.
V. 24, p. 378

KNOWLEDGE

Let us be content to know only what God chooses to reveal.
M. & E., p. 455

In the region of the infinite there is ample space for faith, but reason loses her track; omniscience shall stand instead of personal discovery, infallible revelation in the place of research and argument.
V. 26, p. 511

You will know more after you have been in heaven five minutes than all the doctors of divinity on earth; for there you shall know even as you are known.
V. 26, p. 479

Poor child that I am I would rather love God and wonder at him, than regard him with cold, intellectual apprehension, and dream that I know him altogether.
V. 34, p. 55

I pray for grace to limit my curiosity by the boundaries of God's revelation.
V. 34, p. 55

Knowledge of God far excels all other knowledge as the heavens are higher than the earth.
V. 37, p. 65

He who will not learn more when God is willing to teach him shall forget what he already knows.
V. 46, p. 268

Ignorance is the enemy of faith; but a knowledge of God greatly strengthens and increases our confidence in him.
V. 41, p. 435

The knowledge of God received by a distinct sense of pardoned sin is more certain than knowledge derived by the use of the senses in things pertaining to this life.
V. 34, p. 69

When I know my sin is forgiven, I need no one to say to me, "Know the Lord": the fullness of his pardon has made him known.
V. 34, p. 70

If a man only knows Christ in the head, but does not trust him with the heart, what is the good of his knowledge? It will rather ruin than save him.
V. 23, p. 318

His greatest joy is that those come who, whatever the greatness or littleness of their learning, are childlike in spirit, and like babes are prepared to receive what he shall teach them.
V. 26, p. 678

All the merely human learning that has ever come into the church has, as a rule, been mischievous to it.
V. 26, p. 678

There have been allotted to us times of learning in which we made great acquisitions of knowledge; but "knowledge puffs up," and we were puffed up, I fear.
V. 27, p. 238

"Children of Light" have their eyes opened to a light that shines not from the sun; and they move in an atmosphere in which they behold things which the telescope cannot reveal.
V. 41, p. 236

The aggregate thinking of fallible men is less than nothing when set against the one solitary mind of God.
V. 25, p. 28

God will teach the praying one and he that teaches you to pray will teach you everything else.
V. 61, p. 548

What shall it profit a man if he compass the whole world of knowledge and knows not the way of life.
V. 28, p. 61

Old or young, rich or poor, learned or illiterate, talented or obscure, there is no difference: all believers have everlasting life.
V. 28, p. 65

The powers of mind when rightly exercised upon eternal things, are the means of uplifting us to the highest point to which unaided human nature can attain.
V. 12, p. 97

LAW

You cannot fully preach salvation by Christ without setting Sinai at the back of the picture, and Calvary at the front.
V. 37, p. 48

Men must be made to feel the evil of sin before they will prize the great sacrifice which is the head and front of our gospel.
V. 37, p. 48

Things required by the law are bestowed by the gospel.
V. 28, p. 602

God demands obedience under the law: he works obedience under the gospel.
V. 28, p. 602

God is the author of all law, and it is his will which makes a certain course right, and the contrary to be wrong.
V. 33, p. 272

There is nothing in the Law of God that will rob you of happiness; it only denies you that which would cause you sorrow.
V. 41, p. 305

The Law, as given to Moses, is no longer to us the way of obtaining life, but, in the hands of Christ, it is a most blessed rule for living.
V. 24, p. 628

Our conscience cannot be the standard, the standard is the Law of God.
V. 24, p. 631

LIBERAL THEOLOGY

Negative theology promises no blessing to mankind; it is an empty–handed plunderer, robbing us of every solace, but offering nothing in return.
V. 24, p. 83

If modern thought could be proved to be true the next thing that ought to be done would be to hang the world in sackcloth, because vanity has taken the place of delightful truth.
V. 24, p. 83

I had rather be ridiculed for bigotry than be applauded for "advanced and liberal views."
V. 55, p. 246

If ever there should come a wretched day when all our pulpits be full of modern thought, and the old doctrine of a substitutionary sacrifice shall be exploded, then there will remain no word of comfort for the guilty or hope for the despairing.
V. 32, p. 129

The modern religionist not only hates the doctrine of sovereign grace, but he raves and rages at the mention of it.
V. 37, p. 49

If you remove grace out of the gospel, the gospel is gone,
V. 37, p. 49

We will not bow down to modern thought nor worship the image which human wisdom has set up.
V. 34, p. 344

If you preach a gospel which makes allowances for human nature, and treats sin as if it were a mistake rather than a crime, you will find willing hearers.
V. 37, p. 47

At the very worst, our gospel is better than modern thought at its best.
V. 24, p. 719

There have been thousands who have found their way to hell resting upon the words of some pretended teacher who taught other than the truth.
V. 38, p. 258

LIFE PURPOSE

Do not believe, as the world says, that you must live, there is no absolute necessity for that.
V. 61, p. 114

We must be honest, we must do the right, we must serve God for that is a far greater necessity than that of merely living.
V. 61, p. 114

Many a man who has had next to nothing that could be seen with eyes or handled with hands, has been a very millionaire for true wealth in possessing the kingdom of the Most High.
V. 36, p. 81

Hold everything earthly with a loose hand; but grasp eternal things with a death-like grip.
V. 50, p. 357

Reason teaches us that he who made us, who is our preserver, and at his word we return to dust should be the first object of our thoughts.
V. 13, p. 699

Man is exalted since Christ was humiliated; he may go up to God now that God has come down to man.
V. 13, p. 699

Christ is not sent of God to make you a rich man; he is sent of God to make you a saved man.
V. 42, p. 7

God will never be put in the second place; he must be everything or he will be nothing.
V. 44, p. 594

That I may in all things do what God requires of me, and abstain from everything which he forbids, should be the great object of my life.
V. 24, p. 632

LIQUOR

I abstain myself from alcoholic drink in every form, and I think that others would be wise to do the same.
V. 26, p. 494

LOVE

Nothing teaches us so much the preciousness of the Creator as when we learn the emptiness of all besides.
M. & E., p. 649

Having made Jesus his all, he shall find all in Jesus.
M. & E., p. 705

This great and glorious Being, who fills all things and sustains all things, condescends to rivet upon us—not his pity, mark you, not his thoughts, but the very love of his soul, which is the essence of himself, for he is love.
V. 42, p. 29

We would never have had a spark of love for Jesus if it had not been bestowed upon us by the Divine Spirit.
V. 11, p. 350

God loves men with such omnipotence that at last they hurl their weapons of rebellion down, and submit with eagerness.
V. 23, p. 233

When the world calls us fanatics we are nearing the point of ardour which is our Lord's due.
V. 35, p. 268

Some complain of want of love and are the very people who create that want.
V. 10, p. 106

God loved us better than he loved himself; for, in order that we might live he put himself to that great loss of tearing his Only-begotten from the place of his everlasting abode in peace.
V. 40, p. 39

Do we know one who has less love than others? then let us have more, so as to make up the deficiency.
V. 11, p. 11

In true religion, to love God and to know God are synonymous terms.
V. 17, p. 483

All you have ever been taught from the pulpit, all that you ever studied from the scriptures, all that you have collected from the libraries, all this is no knowledge of God at all unless you love God.
V. 17, p. 483

The worldling loves himself, the Christian loves his God.
V. 21, p. 258

Admit that God ought to be heartily loved, and you are not far from loving him; feel that you are guilty for not loving, and the seeds of love are in your heart.
V. 26, p. 67

God has manifest his love in the death of Christ in a way that must have astonished every inhabitant of heaven.
V. 26, p. 629

He who loves most is the very man who most passionately desires to love more.
V. 26, p. 594

A love that cannot endure a temptation is no love to God at all.
V. 31, p. 665

Love to God is in itself such a delightful emotion that before long the indulgence of it perfumes the whole mind with happiness.
V. 51, p. 666

A mother cries, "Spare my child;" but no mother is more compassionate than our gracious God: He does not afflict willingly, nor grieve the children of men.
M. & E., p. 461

He loved us first, if this is not a good reason for loving him, where could such a reason be found.
V. 60, p. 141

Oh cold hearts! Oh slabs of marble! Oh blocks of granite! Oh icebergs! if we melt not now, when will we melt.
V. 60, p. 141

Let every breath prove it; let every heaving of the lungs, every motion of the tongue and of the hand prove the great and blessed reality of the fact that we love him.
V. 60, p. 137

We cannot love whom we do not know or esteem.
V. 60, p. 134

After we have known Christ by the reading or hearing of the Word, blessed to us by his Holy Spirit, we will be brought into an admiring confidence in him.
V. 60, p. 134

When knowledge has produced faith, that faith gives birth to love.
V. 60, p. 134

Did he lay down his life for us? Ah then beloved, how great must have been his love!
V. 46, p. 2

The more you know the Savior, the better you will love him.
V. 46, p. 535

You can love a man to Christ but you cannot bully him into salvation.
V. 47, p. 27

Is God's love enough for you? It ought to be for if all the loves of husbands, wives, lovers, mothers, fathers, children were distilled, and the quintessence taken out, it would be but water as compared with the generous wine of God's love.
V. 47, p. 381

This light affliction, which is but for a moment, is not worthy to be compared with the exceeding glory of being loved of God.
V. 47, p. 381

The love of Jesus has such a melting power that even a heart of hell–hardened steel softens and flows away in streams of penitence.
V. 32, p. 23

"We love him because he first loved us" is the law of the Christian life.
V. 32, p. 434

Love without beginning is indeed sweet but, there is a more luscious sweetness in love without end.
V. 50, p. 200

Let the love of Christ be believed in and felt in your hearts, and it will humble you.
V. 33, p. 514

If his presence does not cheer you, surely heaven itself would not make you glad; for what is heaven but the full enjoyment of his love.
V. 33, p. 514

The love of Jesus brings joy that is fit for angels, a joy that we shall have continued to us even in heaven, a joy which makes earth like to heaven.

V. 42, p. 161

I have stood by a great many death–beds; but there is one scene I never saw, and never expect to see, that is a child of God repenting that he ever loved Christ Jesus.

V. 42, p. 393

Little as we know compared with what we hope to know, yet his love has become to us the brightest, most conspicuous fact in all our history.

V. 38, p. 94

He began to love us with a love that had no beginning, which has no measure and which shall have no change nor end.

V. 38, p. 104

Ours is a poor little love, not worthy of his acceptance; but such as it is, we give it all to him; and he will not refuse it, or despise it.

V. 38, p. 104

If there were no hereafter, and I had to die like a dog, I would choose to love my God, for I find a peace, a strength, a joy in it that makes life worth living.

V. 41, p. 3

MEDIATOR
❦

You do need a mediator in coming to God but you do not need one in coming to Christ, so go to him just as you are.

V. 5, p. 166

There cannot be any point of contact between absolute deity and fallen humanity except through Jesus Christ, the appointed mediator; that is God's door; all else is a wall of fire.

V. 25, p. 67

MERCY
❧

He who will not have mercy when it is to be had for the asking, deserves to die without it.
V. 13, p. 9

There is not a grain of mercy in the heart of God for that man who continues on in his iniquities.
V. 15, p. 419

What a day that was when the eternal wisdom revealed to man the plan by which the Son of God should suffer instead of us, so that justice might have its claims discharged in full, and yet mercy enjoy its boundless, unlimited sway!
V. 42, p. 5

There is mercy for a sinner, but there is no mercy for the man who will not own himself to be a sinner.
V. 25, p. 62

If mercy shall ever come to you, it will make you a new creation, give you new loves and new hates.
V. 60, p. 41

God's mercy is infinite but it always flows to men through the golden channel of Jesus Christ, his son.
V. 60, p. 42

Beneath the canopy of heaven there cannot be a sinner so abominable that the blood of Christ cannot make a full atonement for all his sins.
V. 60, p. 44

Try to spy out the reason for mercy in God; there is not any reason for it in yourself.
V. 45, p. 465

The sword of justice has less power over human hearts than the scepter of mercy.
V. 28, p. 602

When the Lord has to deal with sincere people, he picks no holes, imputes no motives and dwells on no mistakes.
V. 24, p. 378

We do confess that all our hope lie in divine mercy, for we have no merit.
V. 16, p. 190

I remember how the very grandeur of the divine mercy threatened to crush me down and bury me under its own mass of goodness.
V. 18, p. 69

God will first help the most helpless, and where there is the most misery, there will his mercy most swiftly come.
V. 44, p. 331

It is strange that, when God gives his children mercies, they generally set their hearts more on the mercies than on the Giver of them.
V. 44, p. 99

While we may well suppose that every attribute of God gives him pleasure, mercy is supremely singled out as being especially his favorite.
V. 58, p. 409

The accumulated guilt of all the millions whom Christ redeemed will stand forever as a proof that God delights in mercy.
V. 58, p. 412

Trifle not with sin because God is merciful, this is a cruel, brutal thing to do.
V. 58, p. 415

MYSTERY

What may seem defeat, to us may be victory to him.
M. & E., p. 717

The efficacy of spiritual forces does not depend on our capacity to understand them.

V. 22, p. 270

I look forward to the time when we shall see the knots untied and the riddles all explained: then we shall see the good of apparent evil and the life which lay on the bosom of death.

V. 22, p. 275

The Christian life is a mystery all through, from its beginning to its end; the Christian himself cannot read his own riddle, nor understand himself.

V. 23, p. 312

Who can be astonished at anything, when he has once been astonished at the manger and the cross.

M. & E., p. 53

If even the very hairs of our head are all numbered, if everything be really ordained of the Most High concerning his people, let us rejoice in the divine appointment, and take it as it comes, whether our allotment be rough or smooth, bitter or sweet.

V. 34, p. 54

I do not want to endanger my soul, and perhaps even my reasoning powers, by straining after the unknowable.

V. 34, p. 55

I might be staggered by the divers mysteries which concern theology, which overpower even master–minds, but I confide in Jesus himself.

V. 23, p. 689

The Christian life is a matchless riddle, no worldling can comprehend it.

V. 13, p. 646

Do not expect the world to understand you, Christian, it did not understand your master.

V. 13, p. 646

There are some paradoxes in religion which the world cannot understand; for a man to become a fool that he may be wise, to save his life by losing it, and to be made rich by becoming poor.
V. 55, p. 374

Many among us are perpetually seeking to reconcile truths which probably never can be reconciled except in the divine mind.
V. 12, p. 231 & 232

The will of the Lord is done, and yet the responsibility and freedom of men are left untouched.
V. 30, p. 203

Since revelation is divine, there must be mysteries which mortals cannot understand at present.
V. 37, p. 614

I pray for grace to limit my curiosity by the boundaries of his revelation.
V. 31, p. 55

If you refuse Christ until you understand all mysteries, you will perish in your sins.
V. 13, p. 309

I think, throughout eternity, if we had this problem to solve, why did he call me, we should still go on making wrong guesses.
V. 11, p. 114

There are certain great truths in the Word of God which are hard to be understood; but even those are not difficult because of the language in which they are proclaimed, but because the truth itself is mysterious and deep.
V. 43, p. 425 & 426

OBEDIENCE

Happiness is obedience and obedience is happiness.
V. 47, p. 176

A godly man, who does not yield ready assent to all God's will, ought to pray to be made a godlier man.
V. 47, p. 377

It is all the sweeter to do the Lord's bidding when no trace of personal gain can be found mingling with motive.
V. 36, p. 57

Absolute submission is not enough, we should go on to joyful acquiescence to the will of God.
V. 42, p. 365

We must never bring to God as a sacrifice, a duty smeared with the blood of another duty.
V. 24, p. 630

OLD NATURE

The faith of the flesh is not the faith of God's elect.
V. 17, p. 380

The old nature never does improve, it is earthly and sensual, and devilish in the saint of eighty years of age as it was when he first came to Christ.
V. 17, p. 380

In every one of us it must be fulfilled that all that is of the flesh in us must be withered.
V. 17 p, 375

May the Lord let you see that your goodness is filthiness, that your righteousness is unrighteousness, that the best that is in you is bad, and that the bad that is in you will be your ruin.
V. 18, p. 115

There are too many "retiring" people among us who are so retiring as to get lazy.
V. 40, p. 211

The self–glorification of human nature is foreign to Scripture, which has for its grand object the glory of God.
V. 37, p. 47

The tendency of our proud nature is to cease from childlike confidence in God when once it feels strong enough to rely upon itself.
V. 25, p. 282

All of natures spinning must be unraveled every thread of it must be destroyed.
V. 20, p. 321

If you can provide absolution at small cost and can ease conscience by a little self–denial, it will not be surprising if your religion becomes fashionable.
V. 37, p. 47

When I look back upon my past life, I am horrified at the thought of what I should have come to if God had left me to work out my own righteousness.
Vol. I, p. 333 Autobiography

There is another old man besides old age; and when you begin to feel weary in well doing, may not the old nature have a finger in it as well as the old body.
V. 36, p. 514

He who robs man is called a villain; he who robs God is often called a gentleman.
V. 11, p. 626

PEACE
❦

When consciousness of pardon becomes as strong and vivid as consciousness of guilt, then we enter into the enjoyment of the peace of God which passes all understanding.
V. 24, p. 75

Out of the thick cloud of blackest grief which veils our dying Lord there falls a silver shower of peace, more refreshing than all the brooks of earth can yield.
V. 26, p. 632

What is the reason you do not have peace since you are justified? I will tell you! it is your unbelief.
V. 25, p. 68

There is a peace more precious than the gold of Ophir, there is another peace which is worse than worthless.
V. 36, p. 422

A sinner may say, "I am at peace with God;" but if this comes of forgetting or ignoring him, it is a sorry sham.
V. 36, p. 424

You will never dig peace out of the soil of your own works.
V. 36, p. 429

The more closely you cling to the Lord Jesus, the more clear and full will your peace be.
V. 36, p. 429

As long as your happiness and peace are false, and yet are fair to look upon, you will not seek true peace.
V. 36, p. 431

Do not put up with a false peace, or calm your conscience with anything less than true reconciliation with God.
V. 28, p. 296

Better to be always restless than find rest in a delusion.
V. 28, p. 296

That which men find when they find peace and eternal life is God himself; if men do not find God they have found nothing.
V. 32, p. 496

We dread no annihilation that dark shadow never crosses our spirits; we dread no hell, no purgatory, no judgment; none can condemn whom he absolves.
V. 14, p. 701

A quiet heart, resting in the love of God, dwelling in perfect peace, has a royalty about it which cannot for a moment be matched by the fleeting joys of this world.
V. 14, p. 702

The habit of resignation is the root of peace.
V. 15, p. 222

PERSEVERANCE
❧

According to a certain theology a man may have life in Christ one day and lose it the next; how then is it everlasting life.
V. 28, p. 66

Those who have tender hearts to weep over the sins of their fellows need also brave hearts to stay themselves upon God.
V. 25, p. 277

Beware, dear friends, of the call which makes you set out, but does not lead you to hold out.
V. 14, p. 669

I believe in the final perseverance of every man in whom the regenerating grace of God has wrought a change of nature.
V. 14, p. 670

Eternity shall not reveal a single instance in which Christ Jesus cast away a sinner that came to him.
V. 25, p. 465

We desire to have a flame burning on the heart of our souls which is fed with the fuel of eternal truth and will therefore burn on for evermore.
V. 32, p. 271

We believe in the perseverance of the saints but many are not saints and therefore do not persevere.
V. 35, p. 232

Final perseverance is the test of vital godliness.
V. 55, p. 615

There is no way of killing the life of God when it is once implanted in the heart of a believer in Jesus.
V. 55, p. 620

O you who are a true child of God, you may be drenched, but you shall never be drowned.
V. 45, p. 213

Where is there any ground for confidence if it not be in God who cannot lie and in Christ of the everlasting covenant, and in the Holy Spirit who takes of the things of Christ and reveals them unto us.
V. 45, p. 213

Christ died in the stead of his people, and as God is just, he will never punish one solitary soul of Adam's race for whom the Savior did thus shed his blood.
V. 46, p. 7

If the agonies of the Saviour put our sins away, the everlasting life of the Savior, with the merits of his death added thereto, must preserve his people, even unto the end.
V. 46, p. 7

You cannot take from a man his first birth, neither can you take from a man his second birth; the thought is ridiculous.
V. 24, p. 716

If a man converts you, another man can unconvert you; but if God converts you, I know that what God does shall be forever.
V. 41, p. 259

No union with Christ is living and loving unless it is lasting.
V. 38, p. 105

THE PERSON OF CHRIST

He who does not long to know more of Christ, knows nothing of Him yet.
M. & E., p. 8

Other schools may teach us what is to be believed, but Christ alone can show us how to believe it.
M. & E., p. 19

Let your memory treasure up everything about Christ which you have either felt, or known, or believed, and then let your fond affections hold Him fast for evermore.
M. & E., p. 55

There is not a word which has gone out of the Saviour's lips which he has ever retracted.
M. & E., p. 221

Jesus, be mine forever, my God, my heaven, my all.
M. & E., p. 335

Jesus is not a grain of gold, but a vast globe of it, a priceless mass of treasure such as earth and heaven cannot excel.
M. & E., p. 605

When Jesus was born midnight turned to midday, and when he died midday turned to midnight.
V. 61, p. 374

It is paradise to be with him; and heaven without Christ would be no heaven to me.
V. 11, p. 358

He is God; he can save you; he is man; he is **willing** to save you.
V. 31, p. 222

Trust in his glorious person, in his finished work, in his accepted sacrifice, in his prevailing intercession, and his glorious advent which is yet to be.
V. 30, p. 400

Put out the sun, and light is gone, life is gone, all is gone: when Jesus is pushed into the background the darkness is darkness that might be felt.
V. 23, p. 691

I do not recollect that a single book has been denounced by earnest Christian men because it spoke too highly of the Lord and made him too prominent.
V. 23, p. 691

The splendors of heaven have not made Christ indifferent to the sorrows of earth; he lives to intercede as if this were the express object of his living.
V. 23, p. 653

When through deep distress of mind because you feel yourself to be so unworthy, when you cannot force even a holy groan from your despairing heart, he still pleads for you.
V. 23, p. 655

He makes intercession for the transgressors, then I may venture to believe that he intercedes for me, since I am a transgressor beyond all doubt.
V. 23, p. 65

The whole of the service that he was to render to God, when he came here in human form, was finished in every single part and portion of it.
V. 40, p. 27

If you examine the Master's work and look minutely at every portion of it, the private as well as the public, there is none like it; a multitude of perfections joined together to make up one absolute perfection.
V. 40, p. 27

Men will never spit in his face again; the Romans soldiers will never scourge him again.
V. 40 p. 28

Jesus never wrought a miracle merely for his own comfort.
V. 44, p. 231

I never imagined how strong Christ was till I saw his love held back his Deity! an omnipotence which restrains omnipotence.
V. 44, p. 231

A merely doctrinal religion is pretty sure to degenerate into bigotry; an experimental religion will sooner or later sink into gloom.
V. 60, p. 134

When doctrine and practice and experience all meet in Christ as lines in a centre, then you shall not be degraded, you shall not degenerate.
V. 60, p. 134

If Christ was not God, we are not Christians; we are deceived dupes, we are idolaters, as bad as the heathen whom we now pity.
V. 46, p. 142

Assuredly as long as their was a Father, there was a Son and Jesus Christ has ever been the "Son of the Highest."
V. 47, p. 170

Jesus is God and man in one person: man that he may feel our woes, God that he may help us out of them.
V. 36, p. 499

I do not care two straws what you think of me but I do care a whole world what you think of Christ.
V. 25, p. 192

His love surpasses your knowledge; his goodness, his majesty, his humiliation, his glory, all these transcend your understanding.
V. 25, p. 22

If you plunge deepest into the mystery of the incarnate God you can never reach the bottom of it.
V. 25, p. 22

Our Lord Jesus when on earth was more satisfied by conversing with a poor Samaritan woman than he would have been by the best meat and drink.
V. 16, p. 235

He was very great, and yet he was among them as one who serves.
V. 31, p. 49

He was very wise, but he was gentle as a nurse with her children.
V. 31, p. 49

He was very holy, and far above their sinful infirmities, but he condescended to men of low estate.
V. 31, p. 49

He was the son of the Highest, and nevertheless "a man of sorrows and acquainted with grief."
V. 13, p. 598

He trod the billows of the obedient sea and yet he owned not a foot of land in all Judea.
V. 13, p. 648

He was God in miracles most plenteous but he was man in sufferings most pitiable.
V. 13, p. 698

He is a full Christ for empty sinners.
V. 25, p. 96

He who oversees all worlds as God, was as man, made to sleep, to suffer and to die like ourselves.
V. 18, p. 713

You could not put your finger on one point of his life and say, here he lived for himself alone.
V. 18, p. 23

He was once the king of misery, in that kingdom he reigned supreme: now he is the King of Glory.
V. 14, p. 229

As we stand at the foot of the cross, we feel that every pang he suffered guaranteed to him that he should be King of Kings and Lord of Lords.
V. 14, p. 233

It is heaven to me to think that Christ is in heaven, and another heaven to believe that he will reign among men.
V. 14, p. 238

The Lord Jesus is better than everything that comes from him; his gifts are infinitely precious, then what must he himself be.
V. 42, p. 188

He who was the master of all heaven's majesty came down to be the victim of all man's misery.
V. 21, p. 345

God had one Son without sin, but he never had a son without sorrow and he never will have while the world stands.
V. 38, p. 4

If you deny his Deity, you have sadly destroyed the perfection of his humanity: for a perfect man he could not be if he made me think that he was God when he was not.
V. 38, p. 22

The death of Christ was pre-determined in the counsel of God, and yet it was none the less an atrocious crime on the part of ungodly men.
V. 38, p. 3

Christ is everything to me at all times; a winter Christ and a summer Christ; all my light when I have no other, and all my light when I have every other light.
V. 39, p. 53

By the greatness of his sufferings we may judge of the unspeakable grandeur of his glory.
V. 12, p. 687

There is a style of majestic simplicity about him that is altogether his own, and in this lies unsurpassed sublimity.
V. 31, p. 50

Jesus wept but he never complained.
V. 19, p. 98

Absence from Christ is hell, but presence with Christ is heaven.
V. 8, p. 7

PLEASING GOD

To please God even a little is infinitely better than to have the acclamations of all our race throughout the centuries.
V. 35, p. 454

If you once learn to believe God and to please him, you are coming to him day by day and your life is a march toward him.
V. 35, p. 454

Do you live as near to God now, with that great business to handle, as you did when your hat covered your whole estate, and you went to bed at night with no fear of robbers, for you had nothing to lose.

V. 27, p. 638

PRAYER

You may force your way through anything with the leverage of prayer.

M. & E., p. 105

God keeps a file for our prayers–they are not blown away by the wind, they are treasured in the King's archives.

M. & E., p. 179

The petitions of Moses discomfited the enemy more than the fighting of Joshua, yet both were needed.

M. & E., p. 215

Joshua never grew weary in the fighting, but Moses did grow weary in the praying.

M. & E., p. 215

We can do better without the voice that preaches than without the heart that prays.

V. 37, p. 320

No prayer is half so hearty as that which comes up from the depths of the soul, through deep trials and afflictions.

M. & E., p. 86

A thousand sermons would not prove a man to be a Christian, but one genuine prayer would.

V. 48, p. 583

Much alone, and you will have much assurance; little alone with Jesus, your religion will be shallow, polluted with many doubts and fears and not sparkling with the joy of the Lord.

M. & E., p. 584

Intercession is an honorable service; it is an ennobling thing that a sinner like yourself should be allowed to entreat the King for others.
V. 23, p. 659

Some of the best prayers that have ever been prayed had not a single word to express them, they were heart prayers and went up to heaven in all their naked unclothed glory.
V. 11, p. 560

Many a prayer that has had the choicest words to garnish it, has been nothing but a dead prayer wrapped in grave cloths and only fit to be cast into the grave forever.
V. 11, p. 560

You might as well repeat the multiplication table as repeat the prayer of the day, unless your spirit prays.
V. 11, p. 561

Oh the untold benefits that come to a church from the quiet prayerful members! least known on earth but best known in heaven.
V. 12, p. 539

Brethren, you have many weapons to use with God in prayer, but our Saviour bids you not to neglect this master, all conquering instrument of importunity.
V. 15, p. 108

What showers of blessing come down in answer to the prayers and tears of poor godly invalids, whose weakness is their strength and whose sickness is their opportunity.
V. 15, p. 450

That which is gained speedily by a single prayer is sometimes only a second-rate blessing; but that which is gained after many an awful struggle is a full-rated and precious blessing.
V. 17, p. 601

If they are not saved after twenty years of prayer, follow them, with your prayers, to the gates of hell.
V. 18, p. 140

If God has given us time for secondary duties, he must have given us time for primary ones, and to draw near to him in prayer is a primary duty.
V. 18, p. 140

Since you are tempted without ceasing, pray without ceasing.
V. 18, p. 142

Prayer is the breath of the soul and he that can do without it is dead in sin.
V. 27, p. 128

Go, learn to plead–on when no answer comes, and to press on when repulsed; this is the test of faith.
V. 33, p. 282

When you can pray, and long to pray, why then you will pray; but when you cannot pray and do not wish to pray, why then you must pray, or evil will come of it.
V. 37, p. 91

Cold prayers, so called, are not real prayers; they are rather entreaties to be denied, all their force works backwards.
V. 40, p. 461

Prayer is the catholicon, the universal cure; it subdues every disease, it will unlock the treasures of God and shut the gates of hell.
V. 21, p. 74

Some brethren pray by the yard; but true prayer is measured by weight and not by length.
V. 34, p. 16

When I came to London; there was a slender audience on Sunday, but thank God there was almost as many at the prayer meeting as on the Sunday; and I thought, "this is alright; these people can pray."
V. 21, p. 443

If this were the last word I had to address to this congregation, I would say to you; "dear brethren, abound in prayer, multiply the petitions and the fervour with which you present them to God."
V. 21, p. 444

Pray as you will until the keys of heaven seem to swing at your girdle, yet you can never outrun that omnipotence to bless which dwells in the Lord God Almighty.
V. 21. p. 665

While we live let us be, above all things, men of prayer and when we die, if nothing else can be said of us may men give us this epitaph, which is also our Lord's memorial–"He made intercession for the transgressors."
V. 23, p. 660

If you could perish praying, you would be a new wonder in the universe: a praying soul in hell is an utter impossibility.
V. 35, p. 234

I have heard some Christians say, I do not feel in a proper frame of mind to pray; My brother, pray until you do.
V. 23, p. 280

If you do not pray except when you feel like praying, you will not pray much, nor pray when you most need it.
V. 35, p. 583

Make all your heart known unto God, and keep back nothing, for much benefit will come to you from being honest with your best friend.
V. 26, p. 592

Prayer is the fiery chariot and our desires are its horses of fire.
V. 26, p. 592

O soul, pray even when he does not appear to hear; let nothing stop you from desiring and pouring out your complaint, for herein is the way of health to your spirit.
V. 16, p. 593

A lazy prayer requests a denial and shall have it.
V. 27, p. 573

I always make it a rule to pray for a man when I hear him swear, so in that way, God may bring good out of evil.
V. 51, p. 395

The greater the thing that you ask, the more sure you are to have it.
V. 40, p. 460

There is nothing greater to ask for than Christ, and you shall have Christ for the asking.
V. 40, p. 460

If you ask for wealth you may not get it; for it is a small and paltry thing.
V. 40, p. 460

God is not impoverished by giving and not enriched by withholding.
V. 40, p. 463

A man cannot pray with a good opinion of himself; all he can manage is just to mutter, "God I thank you that I am not as other men are," and that is no prayer at all.
V. 30, p. 351

There are some forms of spiritual life which are not absolutely essential, but prayer is the very essence of spirituality.
V. 14, p. 326

He that has no prayer lacks the very breath of the life of God in his soul.
V. 14, p. 326

Prayers in which there is no thanksgiving are selfish things: they rob God.
V. 14, p. 327

Happy man, happy woman, to have our faith preserved by such a mighty preservative as this—the intercession of Christ.
V. 45, p. 212

We cannot afford to lose the prayer of a single godly child or the most feeble Christian among us.
V. 47, p. 74

Dare we treat the Lord as if he were only to be called upon in our emergencies?
V. 28, p. 290

How can we expect that God will accept prayers that are only forced out of us by selfish fears.
V. 28, p. 290

Let your self–impeachment stand in the forefront of your petition.
V. 28, p. 293

Pray without ceasing not because the circumstances which surround you are favorable, but simply because Jesus bids you to continue in prayer.
V. 28, p. 210

Prayer is the most practical and certain of all the forces that exist this side the eternal throne.
V. 28, p. 642

Whether the prayer be printed or extemporized; unless it comes from the heart, it is equally dead.
V. 50, p. 63

Sometimes words will come at a very rapid rate when there is very little real prayer conveyed by them.
V. 50, p. 64

Prayer is a living thing; you cannot find a living prayer in a dead heart.
V. 50, p. 64

Ananias knew that Saul was a living soul when God said to him, "Behold he prays."
V. 50, p. 64

A man who is self–righteous will not pray, except it be in the fashion of the Pharisee, and that was no prayer at all.
V. 50, p. 65

You might as well say your prayers backward as forward unless your heart goes with it.
V. 50, p. 66

There is a way of merely saying prayers which is rather a mockery of God than a real approach to him as he desires.
V. 50, p. 66

Every true heart–prayer, that is accepted of God first came from God.
V. 50, p. 69

There are no praying souls in hell.
V. 31, p. 701

There is a mysterious efficacy in the prayers of men who dwell near to God.
V. 18, p. 92

How many blessings come down upon the church of God through the prayers of his feeble saints it is not possible for us to tell.
V. 18, p. 93

Prayer gives a channel to the pent–up sorrows of the soul, they flow away and in their place streams of sacred delight pour into the heart.
V. 18, p. 133

Holy joy and prayer act and react upon each other.
V. 18, p. 133

When joy and prayer are married their firstborn child is gratitude.
V. 18, p. 133

Since we are to pray without ceasing, it is clear that audible language is not essential to prayer.
V. 18, p. 134

We may speak a thousand words which seem to be prayer and yet never pray.
V. 18, p. 134

Good men have prayed flat upon their faces, have prayed sitting, standing or any posture and the posture does enter into the essence of the prayer.
V. 18, p. 134

Do not abandon the mercy seat for any reason whatever.
V. 18, p. 136

As long as they live should Christians pray, for only while
they pray do they truly live.
V. 56, p. 49

Preaching is but the wheat–stalk, but praying is the golden
grain itself and he has the best who gets it.
V. 18, p. 140

It is a dreadful thing that we should ever insult the majesty of
heaven by words from which our heart has gone.
V. 18, p. 141

May you go to the throne of God by way of the cross, for that
is the only open way.
V. 18, p. 714

Many kneel apparently in prayer, and not really be praying for
the mind is gadding to and fro.
V. 42, p. 99

In some cases, faith must rise to prayer and must manifest
itself by prayer or it will do nothing.
V. 42, p. 103

The only reason why any man ever begins to pray, is because
God has put previous grace in his heart which leads him to pray.
V. 4, p. 339

I charge you before the living God if you have sought in vain,
do not let Satan make you give it up but ask that Christ will
lead you in the right way.
V. 12, p. 658

PREACHING

Oratory is but a sounding brass or a tinkling cymbal if the
Holy Spirit be not there.
V. 20, 630

When I cease to preach salvation by faith in Jesus put me into a lunatic asylum, for you may be sure my mind is gone.
V. 26, p. 391

If you would preach sinners to Christ you must preach Christ to sinners, for nothing so attracts the hearts of men as Jesus himself.
V. 19, p. 193

That sermon preached in the glory of our oratory turned out to be mere husks for swine; while that discourse which we delivered in weakness, with a humble hope that God would use it, proved to be royal meat for the Lord's chosen.
V. 34, p. 596

For us [ministers] to give ourselves to getting up entertainments, to become competitive with theaters and music halls, is a degradation of our holy office.
V. 37, p. 87

The preaching which only stirs the passions is of small value: we have heard a great deal about crowds weeping, but we had rather see one individual believing.
V. 23, p. 224

One sermon preached in the power of the Holy Spirit will be worth ten thousand preached without it.
V. 35, p. 225

Some talk, "God has a chosen people; therefore I need not preach to them:" no, no, sir; God has a chosen people; therefore I do preach to them.
V. 40, p. 77

Sometimes persons have been led to faith in Christ by feeling that those he sent to be testifiers of his gospel were evidently true to the core and therefore their word was worthy of all acceptation.
V. 18, p. 44

The apostles were honest, unsophisticated men, and they certainly gained nothing by testifying that Christ was the Messiah.
V. 18, p. 44

I fear men will perish, let us preach as we may, while we are regarded as mere orators to be criticized and not as witnesses whose testimony is to be weighed.
V. 18, p. 46

There is a temptation, which assails all of us who preach, to want to do some great thing.
V. 55, p. 555

I abhor all oratory or eloquence except that which comes straight from the heart.
V. 55, p 559

Let us be willing to have our speech called contemptible, as Paul was, for God may then be pleased to bless us as he will not in any other way.
V. 55, p. 559

Some speakers are long in delivering but short on sense; instead of saying much in little, they say little in much.
V. 30, p. 189

Our gospel does not know anything high and low, rich and poor, black and white, cultured and uncultured.
V. 37, p. 48

Preaching is the blast of the rams horn ordained to level Jericho: it is God's choice of fire for bearing souls to heaven and his two edged sword to smite the hosts of hell.
V. 10, 434

Preaching sermons before people is not God's way; we must preach sermons at the people, directly to them.
V. 61, p. 186

I rejoice to preach a gospel that does not borrow strength from me, but gets its power from God.
V. 45, p. 315

Better that the sun should not rise than that Christ be not preached.
V. 45, p. 278

That woman (Mary of Bethany) has been a preacher to nine-
teen centuries; the influence of that alabaster box is not
exhausted today, and never will be.
V. 36, p. 59

Our reply to the outcry about the failure of the pulpit is to get
into it and preach with the Holy Spirit sent down from heaven.
V. 28, p. 212

What to one is an appropriate word of encouragement, may
be to another an equally suitable word of rebuke.
V. 32, p. 497

The preacher sent of God is an echo of God's voice.
V. 24, p. 59

Often I have heard inquirers say, "It seemed to me as if that
sermon was meant for me, there were points in it which were
so exactly like myself that I felt sure someone had told the
preacher about me."
V. 16, p. 165

It is never worth a minister's while to go into his pulpit to
show his listeners that he is adept in elocution.
V. 15, p. 278

The Saviour ignored all idea of beautiful expression in just
bringing forth his meaning in the plainest possible manner.
V. 31, p. 50

Learned men will not stoop to common place things; they
must say something great, sublime, dazzling, brilliant and "full
of fireworks."
V. 31, p. 50

The minister can get into a way of preaching that is almost
like a parrot repeating by rote what it is taught to say.
V. 42, p. 99

If preaching is not a supernatural exercise, it is a
useless procedure.
V. 38, p. 117

Knowing the terrors of the Lord, we persuade; knowing the joys of true religion we entreat.
V. 35, p. 325

God's servant is not to preach smooth things, but true things.
V. 43, p. 440

That sermon which pleases us most, may not profit us at all; while the one which grieves and annoys us may, perhaps, be doing us a most essential service.
V. 44, p. 323

You have never heard a really quickening word from my lips alone: it may have come, perhaps, through my mouth as the vocal organ: but if it be a quickening word it must have come from God himself.
V. 32, p. 497

Multitudes of sermons are preached, very zealously, to propagate falsehoods, sea and land are compassed to make proselytes who shall be ten times more children of hell than they were before.
V. 61, p. 115

PRIDE

Nothing is more deadly than self–righteousness or more hopeful than contrition.
M. & E., p. 115

He who boasts of grace has little grace to boast of.
M. & E., p. 148

May infinite wisdom cure us from the madness of self–confidence.
M. & E., p. 153

Some professors (of religion) are sharper than a thorn hedge; such men are not like Jesus.
M. & E., p. 291

Lord, keep us in old age, when becoming conceited of our wisdom we may prove greater fools than the young and giddy.
M. & E., p. 363

Man never could or would have invented a gospel which would lay him low, and give to the Lord God all the glory and praise.
V. 37, p. 47

He that is his own master has a fool and a tyrant to be his Lord.
V. 17, p. 438–439

Beware of mock humility; much that we say about ourselves would mightily offend us if anybody else said the same of us.
V. 17, p. 269

It will never do for us to be satisfied with ourselves, for vehement love thinks nothing is good enough for Christ.
V. 86, p. 332

Pride is a cunning thing, it lives to wear the robes of a prince, but if it cannot, it is satisfied to wear the rags of a beggar.
V. 12, p. 66

I am more afraid of a lofty pride of self than of anything else under heaven.
V. 44, p. 489

You may hunt down this fox and think you have destroyed it, and lo! your very exaltation is pride.
V. 29, p. 421–422

None have more pride than those who dream they have none.
V. 24, p. 421–422

The self–righteous man knows that what he is doing cannot satisfy God, for it cannot satisfy himself.
V. 15, p. 346

Pride is the associate of presumption, but humility is the companion of assurance.
V. 16, p. 346

Self–reliance is well enough in matters of the world, but self–reliance is absolute madness in the things of God.
V. 18, p. 111

The easiest way to give resurrection to old corruptions is to erect a trophy over their graves.
V. 19, p. 309

If you put the praise of men before the approval of God, you are in an evil case.
V. 35, p. 427

Any notion of our own attainment which could lead us for a moment to speak of what we are with any degree of complacency is only rubbish.
V. 20, p. 82

Of all estimates of ourselves, that which is founded upon our apparent usefulness is likely to be the most deceptive.
V. 22, p. 605–606

A man may escape from a great blunder, and yet if he grows proud because he was so prudent, it may happen that his conceit of his own wisdom may be a worse evil than the mistake which he might have made.
V. 26, p. 269

Is there ever a time when a man is so proud as when he judges that he is humble?
V. 26, p. 515

Righteous men know themselves to be sinners, sinners believe themselves to be righteous.
V. 37, p. 53

Do you see any spiritual beauty in yourself? then it is because you do not know what true beauty is.
V. 22, p. 8

Boasters are hardly conscious of their own falsehoods, for they have talked themselves into believing their own bombast.
Proverbs & Sayings, p. 4

Many a man is more a slave to his admirers than he dreams of: the love of approbation is more a bondage than an inner dungeon would be.
V. 36, p. 591

He that goes tramping through his Christian career as if he were somebody, and all were safe, is no favorite of heaven.
V. 35, p. 107

Honour gained by a heartless profession of faith is, in God's sight the greatest disgrace.
V. 35, p. 306

The self–righteous care nothing for pardon though it cost the Redeemer his life's blood.
V. 55, p. 381

What proud wretches we must be, pride must be ingrained in us, if we need all this discipline to get it out.
V. 40, p. 44

Unbelief is only a kind of veiled pride in which we begin to set up our own judgment against the wisdom of God.
V. 40, p. 44

Until self–confidence is emptied out of us there is no room for confidence in God.
V. 40, p. 45

I cannot help bearing my testimony that I am greatly afraid of any men who make loud profession of superior sanctity.
V. 19, p. 304

There are some people who would be excellent Christians if Christianity consisted in having their own way and gaining honor for themselves.
V. 47, p. 176

We are all, by nature, as proud as Lucifer.
V. 47, p. 38

Nothing will ever cover up our pride except our winding sheets; and when our bodies are wrapped up in them, and our souls are caught up to dwell with God, then, but not till then, shall pride be thoroughly cast out of us.
V. 47, p. 38

There is no legitimate cause for pride in any of us; and therefore, God, to keep his people in their right place, humbles them with discoveries of their own sinfulness.
V. 47, p. 39

Sometimes your good works have been a great evil to you, because you have prided yourself upon them, and so brought yourself to the edge of the precipice of presumption.
V. 47, p. 39

The Lord Jesus has not come to save you proud and arrogant ones, who sit on your thrones and look down contemptuously on others.
V. 36, p. 90

Men seek not the light, because they boast that they are the children of the day and need no light from above.
V. 28, p. 20

It is easy to be proud while sneering at pride and glorying in self while denouncing all self-exaltation.
V. 24, p. 14

To be proud of our association with the great ones of the earth, is both a folly and a sin on the part of any child of God.
V. 50, p. 91

If ever you meet with a hard–hearted proud man, he is not a happy man and if he should seem to be happy it is a dangerous happiness.
V. 22, p. 35

Let us never attempt to show off, or make ourselves somebody, or exhibit our strength of faith.
V. 31, p. 49

People will say in prayer, "thy poor dust" and use all kinds of depreciating expressions, when they are as proud as Lucifer.
V. 13, p. 247

May the Lord pump you dry of all your self–sufficiency, and then the stream of eternal mercy will come flowing down through the silver pipe of the atoning sacrifice, and you shall rejoice and live.
V. 12, p. 108

Some of our brethren are very anxious to carry out the decrees of God, instead of believing that God can carry them out himself.
V. 11, p. 495

Some people say, "You know it is a natural pride, as if it being a natural pride made it any better.
V. 43, p. 126

If any of you are so high and mighty that you must go to heaven fashionably, you will be lost.
V. 43, p. 436

The self glorification of human nature is foreign to scripture, which has for its object the glory of God.
V. 37, p. 47

PROCRASTINATION

Now is the only time worth having, because indeed it is the only time we have.
V. 32, p. 80

To live one hour apart from Christ is to live in infinite peril, since in that hour you may die, and pass beyond the realms of hope.
V. 33, p. 509

PROMISE
❦

If one promise of God to one of his people should fail, that one failure would mar the veracity of the Lord to all eternity; they would publish it in the "Diabolical Gazette, " and in every street of Tophet they would howl it out, "God has failed."
V. 34, p. 343

PROPHESY
❦

I believe in the restoration of the Jews to their own land in the last days.
V. 55, p. 170

Before Jesus Christ shall come upon this earth again, the Jews shall be permitted to go to their beloved Palestine.
V. 55, p. 170

We read the twenty–second Psalm, and if we did not know that it had been composed many, many years before our Lord came, we should look at it as history rather than prophecy.
V. 60, p. 112

The Jewish people have been scattered throughout all nations, they shall be restored to their own land.
V. 16, p. 241

The nonsense of modern pretenders to prophesy is no writing of God.
V. 28, p. 606

PROSPERITY
❦

Men may drown in seas of prosperity as well as rivers of affliction.
M. & E., p. 495

The Christian far oftener disgraces his profession in prosperity than in adversity.
M. & E., p. 82

Yet this failure is not a matter of necessity, for the apostle tells us that he knew how to abound.
M. & E., p. 82

We possess nothing here; the goods which we think we possess melt away like an icicle in a hot hand.
V. 34, p. 462

We are so constituted that we cannot bear very much prosperity.
V. 27, p. 638

When God favors a man with prosperity he will send a corresponding amount of affliction to go with it, to deprive it of its injurious tendencies.
V. 27, p. 639

Saints are poor sometimes; but they do not know the poverty of the man who has no God.
V. 40, p. 38

It is a blessed thing to have God when you have all things beside, and find God in all things; but it is an equally blessed thing to have God when you have nothing else and to find all things in him.
V. 40, p. 38

PROVIDENCE

If not a sparrow falls upon the ground without your Father; you have reason to see that the smallest events of your career are arranged by him.
V. 15, p. 462

The Lord cannot be unkind to me in providence; for it is impossible that he can forsake those whose names are upon the palms of his hands.
V. 19, p. 261

There is one who rules over all, who, without complicity in their sin, makes even the actions of wicked men to serve his holy and righteous purpose.

V. 20, p. 623

I bless the Lord for the correction of his providence by which he has blessed men on one hand with sweets, he has blessed me on the other hand with bitters.

V. 27, p. 639

When believers get to heaven, and look back on their own pathway on earth, they will admire the amazing lovingkindness and unerring wisdom of God in arranging all that they have passed through.

V. 54, p. 39

He knows the end from the beginning, and will not allow the flood of human iniquity to swell beyond the control of his supreme will.

V. 34, p. 666

You shall find that God has appointed with exact wisdom, with profound knowledge, and with irreproachable love all the days and doings of your life.

V. 13, p. 435

Empires rise and flourish, they flourish but to decay, they rise to fall.

V. 3, p. 309

Sometimes that which appears to be a great mistake may, nevertheless, in the hand of God, prove to be the right course.

V. 62, p. 367

REGENERATION

The heart must be entirely renewed by a miracle of mercy, such as can only be wrought by that omnipotent hand which made heaven and earth.

V. 28, p. 606

In regeneration lies the essence and major portion of resurrection.
V. 28, p. 67

When he made the world it was with a word, but in the making of a Christian it needs the labour of the Godhead.
V. 25, p. 188

RELIGION

Some take religion to be simply the indulgence of their tastes, the pleasing of the eye or the gratification of the senses.
V. 61, p. 380

If they can sit while the pealing organ pours forth floods of music and they are charmed thereby, they call that adoration.
V. 61, p. 380

The gratification of the senses, of the ear and the eye cannot be devotion.
V. 61, p. 380

In the case of all other religions, the preaching to the gentiles is absent.
V. 13, p. 704

Let any other faith than the Christian show me a man traversing alone the center of Africa like Livingston, or dwelling alone with bushman as Moffet has done.
V. 13, p. 704

O you heathen, if your religions be true, why do you not promulgate them?
V. 13, p. 704

There is much of religion, nowadays, that is very superficial, it is all on the surface.
V. 41, p. 304

REPENTANCE
❦

There is a repentance that needs to be repented of.
V. 8, p. 581

There is a remorse which is near akin to repentance, but it is not the fruit of the grace of God.
V. 55, p. 560

The soul which is enlightened with His Spirit, can tell whether the repentance be genuine or not.
V. 8, p. 581

I can understand a child of God saying, "I am out of fellowship with Christ," but I cannot understand his saying that calmly and deliberately, without tears, without deep regret and intense repentance.
V. 20, p. 365

If I was asked whether a man repented first, or believed first, I should reply, "which spoke of the wheel moves first when the wheel starts."
V. 47, p. 426

Where there is repentance there is faith already, for the two never can be separated.
V. 9, p. 532

Learn this lesson—not to trust Christ because you repent, but to trust Christ to make you repent; not to come to Christ because you have a broken heart but to come to him to give you a broken heart.
V. 47, p. 424

Holy sorrow for sin is as indispensable as faith.
V. 21, p. 123

A dry–eyed faith is no faith at all.
V. 21, p. 123

Ask yourself if you have that which is repentance unto life, for you may humble yourself for a time, and yet never repent before God.

V. 1, p. 333

Sincere repentance is continual: believers repent until their dying day.

M. & E., p. 574

If you tell me that there can be such a thing as spiritual repentance and yet no sorrow for having broken the law of God, I tell you that you do not know what you are talking about.

V. 46, p. 424

Sorrow for sin is a perpetual rain, a sweet soft shower which, to a truly gracious man, lasts all his life long.

V. 46, p. 425

True sorrow for sin must be blended with a child–like submission to God, and consequent confidence in Christ; otherwise it is not "godly sorrow."

V. 46, p. 429

True repentance is sorrow for the sin itself, it has not only the dread of death which is the wages of sin, but of sin which earns the wages.

V. 35, p. 1223

The man who only repents of this or that glaring offense, has not repented at all.

V. 35, p. 124

When you have grown too big for repentance, depend upon it, you have grown too proud for faith.

V. 35, p. 130

Faith cheers repentance, and repentance sobers faith.

V. 35, p. 424

You who do not like self–examination are the persons who need it most.

V. 35, p. 424

It is easy to bring a man to the river of regret, but you cannot make him drink of the water of repentance.
V. 10, p. 100

If you remain unconverted, you may go from bad to worse, heaping sin upon sin, and you heart will get harder and harder until you are given up to final impenitence.
V. 55, p. 561

He that can see his own deformities, shall not be long before he sees the Lord's unspeakable perfections.
V. 51, p. 77

That repentance which is the work of the flesh will need to be repented of.
V. 17, p. 380

Repentance is the daily and hourly duty of a man who believes in Christ.
V. 8, p. 406

I do not believe in the faith that is unaccompanied by repentance.
V. 54, p. 257

Some seem to jump into religion as if they were going into a bath, and then jump out again just as quickly.
V. 54, p. 257

Faith and repentance are twins, they are born together, and they will live together.
V. 54, p. 257

God would have you know in your heart the guilt of sin by bitterly lamenting it.
V. 61, p. 234

I do not know, beloved, when I am more perfectly happy than when I am weeping for sin at the foot of the cross.
V. 60, p. 234

I learn from the Scriptures that repentance is just as necessary for salvation as faith is.
V. 46, p. 246

To mourn over sin, and struggle against it and try to overcome it: this is a sure mark of grace; a far surer one than overflowing joy.

V. 36, p. 616

The non–repentance prophets cry, "Peace, peace" when there is no peace.

V. 28, p. 502

A man must be driven to self–despair before he will agree to be saved by faith in Christ.

V. 28, p. 69

If you know something of your failure the Lord will lead you further.

V. 28, p. 309

An eye that glistens with the tears of penitence is a far greater marvel than the cataract of Niagara.

V. 16, p. 337

True repentance is the gift of the Holy Spirit, and when it is sought of the Lord, it is never denied.

V. 18, p. 53

If you cannot come to Christ with a broken heart, come for a broken heart, for it is his gift.

V. 18, p. 53

The day will come when inasmuch as you have rejected the easy yoke of repentance, you will have to bear the iron yoke of remorse.

V. 18, p. 58

If you repent of your sins, you have not committed the unpardonable sin, since that sin necessitates hardness of heart.

V. 11, p. 607

Every failure should cause me sorrow and every mistake should lead me to chasten myself with penitence.

V. 24, p. 632

REST
℘

Ambition spoils rest.
V. 23, p. 31

Impatiently coveting more than God is pleased to give, ruins rest.
V. 23, p. 31

The labour of love for Christ is only another word for rest.
V. 35, p. 334

We do not mean sleep or idleness when we speak of rest: that is not rest but rust.
V. 35, p. 334

Can there ever be rest for the race who were driven out of Paradise?
V. 15, p. 217

Is rest possible for a soul polluted with sin tossed to and fro with inward lust and agitated with outward temptations?
V. 15, p. 217

Man without God is like the mariner in the story, condemned to sail on forever, and never to find a haven.
V. 15, p. 217

A believing soul is never more at ease that when she is putting forth her full strength in the service of God.
V. 15, p. 221

It is neither in our sanctification, nor our usefulness, nor our conformity that we find rest—our rest comes through believing in Christ.
V. 15, p. 224

You obtain it by believing and you keep it by believing.
V. 15, p. 228

It is his way to lead his people into the wilderness when he means ultimately to bring them into the rest of Canaan.
V. 41, p. 318

We should be in a most unrestful state if we had nothing to do; we should be worn out with the weariness of living an aimless, purposeless life.
V. 58, p. 135

The truest state of rest is when a man has just as much to do as he can perform with ease.
V. 58, p. 135

Heaven is a place of perfect rest, yet it is not the rest of stagnation; they serve God continually and that is perfect rest.
V. 58, p. 135

I do not believe that God finds rest in the Baptist denomination or in the independent or the church of England; he finds His rest in those whom his grace has called whatever the denomination.
V. 58, p. 139

RESURRECTION

The resurrection will be to the body what regeneration has been to the soul.
V. 33, p. 226

This poor world dimly guessed at the immortality of the soul, but it knew nothing of the resurrection of the body.
V. 14, p. 701

It would not be a complete victory over sin and Satan, if the Saviour left part of his people in the grave and only emancipated their spirits.
V. 18, p. 470

REVERENCE

There is a holy familiarity with God which cannot be too much enjoyed; but there is a flippant familiarity with God that cannot be too much abhorred.
V. 37, p. 159

Fanaticism is a tornado of the flesh, and not the health–giving breath of the Holy Spirit.
V. 37, p. 92

Enoch walked with God, he did not run with him.
V. 37, p. 92

The wild fury of the flesh, in which everything is done by noise, and men are saved by bluster, is not of God.
V. 37, p. 92

The excitement of animal enthusiasm will die out like the crackling of thorns under a pot.
V. 32, p. 271

Excitement may sometimes be used of God to stir the spirit of man, but unless your religion is based on something more than animal excitement it is based on a lie.
V. 11, p. 439

That devotion which must always show itself by shouting may be very genuine but it is to be feared that it is superficial.
V. 35, p. 118

Sitting silently at his feet in lowliest reverence is of more worth than all the clatter of Martha's dishes.
V. 35, p. 119

When we fall at his feet in lowliest reverence of joyful love, we become doubt–proof.
V. 35, p. 119

Communion with God bows a man to the dust and causes him to use lowly and reverent language.
V. 37, p. 495

God never comes near to us and then leave us in a frame of mind in which we could speak flippantly or irreverently of him.
V. 37, p. 495

Your humblings are nothing but another form of pride unless your souls have a reverent and deep respect unto the Lord.
V. 13, p. 244

Affection must not degenerate into familiarity: he must be reverenced as well as loved.
V. 14, p. 60

REVIVAL
ॐ

One-half of the emotions excited in our places of worship are of no more value than those excited at the theater.
V. 11, p. 559

Animal excitement is based upon a lie and shall be nothing more than the blowing up of a bubble, which shall burst and leave not a vestige behind.
V. 11, p. 559

Plead more earnestly in private, make your prayer meetings more energetic, attend them more numerously, throw your hearts more fully into them, and God's Spirit will be surely given.
V. 20, p. 23

It is hard living in a careless state in the midst of revival.
V. 23, p. 307

The wild–fire and madness of some revivals have been a perfect disgrace to the common sense of the age, let alone the spirituality of the church.
V. 10, p. 613

We are agreed brethren, that we do not want sinners to be converted by our persuasion, or brought into the church by excitement; we want the Spirit's work and the Spirit's work alone.
V. 10, p. 617

Lord, if this is our work, end it; if it is man's work, break it down; but if it be your work, revive it.
V. 25, p. 287

This is good pleading: "It is your work, we cannot do it, we will not attempt to do it; but, Lord, it is yours, you must do it, we hold you to it by humble faith."
V. 25, p. 287

Christianity has flourished among the despised poor when it has been rejected by the great ones of the earth.
V. 25, p. 28

None of us can remember the early Methodist days; they were over before we were born; but they were very wonderful times when the preaching of the Word was like fire in the midst of the people.
V. 41, p. 386

When He has insulted all pride, dimmed all human glory, and magnified himself, then indeed we have times of refreshing from his presence.
V. 51, p. 81

In revival, every action shall be filled with vigour, every thought shall glow with earnestness, every word shall be clothed with divine power.
V. 10, p. 614

REWARD

I believe the Lord will give to the sick and the suffering an equal reward with the active and energetic, if they are equally concerned for his glory.
V. 37, p. 320

He will reward you, not according to your success, but according to the measure of grace which you use faithfully in his service.
V. 59, p. 138

A little while of witness bearing, a little while of suffering, a little while to be rebuked, and then "forever with the Lord."
V. 10, p. 375

The "well–done, good and faithful servant," from the Master's own lips is worth ten thousand thunders of applause from senators and princes.
V. 30, p. 377

The Father has called us to have fellowship with Christ, and to be partakers of all that he has.
V. 11, p. 118

The garden of Eden, fair as were its glades, and lovely as were its flowers, was but a faint image of the things prepared for man had he continued in loyalty to God.
V. 24, p. 61

RICHES

What a sad thing it is that so many are rich in all things except the one thing needful.
V. 28, p. 15

A man is truly rich who has a good help–meet.
V. 42, p. 139

Prosperity is not always a token of blessing; it may be the proof of the Lord's favor and it may not be.
V. 38, p. 16

God sometimes gives most to those on earth who will have nothing in heaven.
V. 38, p. 16

If you have been hindered in growing rich I should set that down to the good providence of God.
V. 11, p. 609

RIGHTEOUSNESS

We are endowed with a righteousness, not of our own performing, but of his imputing.
V. 61, p. 188

Beware of surface godliness; there must be in us a hungering and a thirsting after righteousness.
V. 60, p. 41

There is no such thing as human righteousness: the two words make up a contradiction.
V. 36, p. 515

We have no personal merit, but we are justified by imputed righteousness.
V. 36, p. 515

You are covered with his righteousness, and heaven itself cannot provide a robe more spotless.
V. 36, p. 74

RITUAL
❧

Ritual performances are very pretty spectacles for silly young ladies, and sillier men to gaze upon, but there is no shadow of spirit or life in them.
V. 11, p. 563

Garments, genuflections, rituals, oblations and the like are ignored; the Lord's eye of favor rests only upon hearts broken and humbled before him.
V. 55, p. 376

Of what use is the laying on of hands? Full often, I fear it is only empty hands laid on empty heads.
V. 45, p. 246

SACRIFICE
❧

The most difficult thing was not for Pharaoh to be compelled to let the people go, but to bring the people into such a state of mind that they would be willing to quit the fertile land.
V. 32, p. 435

Unless your religion tears you away from yourself, and makes you live for something nobler than even your own spiritual good, you have not passed out of darkness into the light of God.
V. 32, p. 359

The removal of one man is often the opportunity for the springing up of scores of others to do equal service.
V. 24, p. 128

If you are a loser because of conscience, the Lord will pay you back, not with silver of earthly prosperity, but with the gold of spiritual joy.
M. & E., p. 353

SALVATION

Salvation by works of the law is a frail and broken vessel whose shipwreck is sure.
M. & E., p. 623

While the story of King Manasseh stands on record, no mortal has a just excuse to perish in despair; no one is justified in saying, "God will never forgive me."
V. 40, p. 441

As surely as your overthrow was inconceivably terrible, so the designs of God for your redemption are inconceivably magnificent.
V. 46, p. 501

Remember that whatever may be against you–whatever may have defiled you–however black, however filthy, however worthless you may be, you are invited to take of the fountain of the water of life freely.
V. 22, p. 17

I thank God that he does not bless the sins of his people, for if he did it would bring on them the tremendous curse of being happy in the ways of evil.
V. 20, p. 352

Pardon is given to penitent sinners on the basis of justice, as well as mercy, because of the pains and grief and agonies of the Divine Redeemer.
V. 11, p. 418

In the great Romish Church there are hundreds of thousands who have found the Saviour, and are resting on his atoning sacrifice; these are God's hidden ones.

V. 40, p. 306

Not our wounds, but his wounds; not our griefs but his griefs, not our tears, but his blood must save us; away, therefore, forever with the notion that there is a certain point of grief that has to be reached to qualify us for coming to the Saviour.

V. 46, p. 425

All your church goings, and all your sayings of prayers, and all your reading of the Bible are of no value in his sight unless your heart is right with him.

V. 49, p. 304

Child of God: every promise is yours, Christ is yours, God is yours, the Holy Spirit is yours, this world is yours and the world to come, time is yours, eternity is yours, life is yours, death is yours; everlasting glory is yours.

V. 21, p. 92

We were dead in sin and far from God, and he surprised us with his preventing mercy, and in us was fulfilled the words, "I was found of them that sought me not.

V. 21, p. 668

If you had saved yourself, that poor work of yours would, like all man's work, one day pass away; but salvation is of the Lord, and therefore it will stand forever.

V. 23, p. 343

I was in my own esteem the blackest of sinners, and sunk in the depth of despair, yet I believed, and by that faith I leaped into a fullness of light and liberty at once.

V. 24, p. 454

The first work of grace in the heart does not begin with man's desire, but with God's planting the desire.

V. 11, p. 640

There was never a man yet who, with all his heart, did seek the Lord Jesus Christ, but sooner or later found him.
V. 46, p. 246

The third (chap.) of Genesis reveals ruin; the third of Romans teaches redemption; the third of John sets forth regeneration.
V. 36, p. 517

Our misery is our own work, but our salvation is of the Lord.
V. 28, p. 22

Human salvations are the gift of works; divine salvation is the gift of grace.
V. 32, p. 435

At this moment God's omnipresent heart beats in sympathy with all our hearts if we are seeking his love.
V. 32, p. 496

Every lost soul needs a thousand things; but no soul needs more than it will find in God.
V. 32, p. 496

If he is found of those who seek him not (Rom. 10:20), he will surely be found by those who are daily agonizing for him.
V. 32, p. 504

We are inclined to think that natural miracles are greater than spiritual ones, that the dividing of the Red Sea is a greater miracle than forgiving of sins, but the spiritual miracle is infinitely greater.
V. 50, p. 195

What a task we undertake in trying to win one soul, much more in seeking to win a city or the world for Christ.
V. 42, p. 113

If you wish to save yourselves, do it, but God will have no share in the work.
V. 57, p. 379

If God is to save you, he must be Alpha and Omega; he must have all the praise because he gives all the power.
V. 57, p. 379

SANCTIFICATION

Let not the hope of perfection hereafter make us content with imperfection now.
M. & E., p. 273

The overruling hand of the Master is accomplishing the purity of the grain by the very process which the enemy intended to be destructive.
M. & E., p. 344

It is not needful that I should be rich, but it is imperative upon me that I be pure.
M. & E., p. 414

The most golden faith or the purist degree of sanctification to which a Christian ever attained on earth, has still so much alloy in it as to be only worthy of the flames, in itself considered.
M. & E., p. 603

It is better to have the cross sanctified than removed.
M. & E., p. 617

When I hear of anybody of angry spirit losing his temper, I always pray that he may not find it again, for such tempers are best lost.
V. 53, p. 545

Why should not you and I dear friends, always be consciously in the presence of God? We are never right unless we are in that condition.
V. 53, p. 180

He that is most conscious of life in Christ, is also most convinced of his own death apart from Christ.
V. 34, p. 15

If you have a faith in Christ which does not make you desire holiness it is a delusion that will drag you to the bottomless pit.
V. 12, p. 37

To mourn after greater conformity to the image of Christ proves that we are already, in a measure, conformed thereto.
V. 17, p. 581

Your soul even though it cannot be perfect in action, at any rate can be perfect in aim.
V. 18, p. 412-413

Better to feel a heavenly hunger than a worldly fullness.
V. 27, p. 129

Growing Christians think themselves less than nothing.
V. 21, p. 548

Until you die, you will have some evil to struggle with and as long as you are in this body, there will be enough tinder for one of the devil's sparks to set it alight.
V. 57, p. 58

Revenge is not a word that ought to be found in Christian's dictionary.
V. 53, p. 546

The man who cannot learn anymore is the man who never learned anything aright.
V. 21, p. 544

A perfectly Christ–like soul finds all the world too narrow for its abode, for it lives and loves; it lives by loving, and loves because it lives.
V. 35, p. 347

Some Christians overlook the blessing of sanctification and yet to a thoroughly renewed heart this is one of the sweetest gifts of the covenant.
T.D. V. 1, p. 400

The Christian, if he should ever come to perfection, and God grant we each may come as near to it as possible, will find the old "I" kept under and the new Christ–like reigns supreme.
V. 13, p. 647

We ought to be ashamed, brethren if we allow those sins to conquer us now which overcame us years ago.
V. 26, p. 634

We ought to possess a growing strength against iniquity, a growing abhorrence of evil and a growing likeness to Christ.
V. 26, p. 634

Living desires are better than dead duties, as a living dog is better than a dead lion.
V. 26, p. 596

A man of devotion is always a man of desires; the best people are fullest of longings to be better.
V. 26, p. 597

Covetousness of goods is a crime, but covetousness of good is a virtue.
V. 26, p. 597

It is a wicked error to conceive that so much of life ought to be religious and so much to be secular.
V. 25, p. 274

A Christian's whole life is to be his religion, and his religion is to saturate his whole life.
V. 25, p. 274

He who bought us with his precious blood did not buy us with a reserve and leave the devil with a mortgage upon us.
V. 25, p. 274

I would not like to have an unconsecrated hair on my head, or an unconsecrated hour of the day, or an unconsecrated faculty.
V. 20, p. 165

If Christ finished the work for us, he will finish the work in us.
V. 40, p. 31

Rough material as you are, he can make you what you should be; he can make you what it will delight you to be.
V. 31, p. 149

The good which God works in his people must be good always and can never be described as bad.
V. 11, p. 646

We are to groan after perfection, but we are to wait patiently for it, knowing what the Lord appoints is best.
V. 14, p. 11

There is heaven in this {groaning}, and though the word sounds like sorrow, there is a depth of joy concealed within.
V. 14, p. 11

Spiritual growth, if we have any, must never be the subject of our self–congratulation, we must give all the glory to God.
V. 61, p. 235

There is a vast difference between grace growing and growing in grace.
V. 46, p. 530

A sense of satisfaction with yourself will be the death of your progress, and will prevent your sanctification.
V. 44, p. 20

While grace cannot grow more, we can grow more in it, and so we shall grow in grace.
V. 46, p. 521

Some saints progress further in grace in one single month than others do in twelve months or twelve years.
V. 46, p. 532

There is not an instance in sacred scripture of a young man disgracing his profession; but there are instances of men of middle age and gray hairs doing so.
V. 46, p. 532

Many of God's plants grow best in the dark, and he often puts them in the dark to make them grow.
V. 46, p. 533

Let me urge you not to think you are growing in grace because you happen to be doing a little more for the church externally.
V. 46, p. 534

A man may have his hands ever so full before the world and think he is doing much, but he may not be really growing in grace after all.
V. 46, p. 534

It happens that, when we are very full of public labours, we are short in private devotions.
V. 46, p. 534

Large numbers of God's people are contented with a very poor form of spiritual life, because they do not think it possible to advance farther.
V. 36, p. 509

Do not let us live according to our natural quality, but let us live according to our supernatural elevation.
V. 36, p. 510

The Lord has done great things for you when every evil thing is obnoxious to you.
V. 28, p. 608

Drop yourselves like plastic clay at the potters feet, and he will put you on the wheel and mold you at his pleasure.
V. 25, p. 191

God forgives the sin that he may purify the sinner.
V. 33, p. 381

Sanctification must not be forgotten or overlaid by justification.
V. 18, p. 13

Men will never know us by our faith, for that is within us; they know us by our works, which are visible to them.
V. 18, p. 23

He who shakes the earth with earthquakes and sweeps the sea with tornadoes, can send a heartquake and a storm of strong repentance, and tear up your old habits by the roots.
V. 14, p. 153

If God is anything we ought to make him everything; you cannot put God in the second place.
V. 38, p. 242

If every part of you is not consecrated to Christ, I fear that no part of you is consecrated to him.
V. 38, p. 439

Rest wholly and alone upon Christ: say "I rest in him, whether I am a saint or a sinner, whether I am useful or defeated in my service.
V. 39, p. 53

We cannot live too near to Christ; the very marrow of religion lies in that which some men think to be the great precision of it.
V. 43, p. 427

The full enjoyment of true religion does not belong to the great mass of Christian professors; they do not get near enough to the center and heart of it to realize what its sweetness is.
V. 43, p. 427

Some people think so much about their own sanctification that they miss sanctification altogether.
V. 44, p. 117

Has he who made you launched you forth on the tempestuous sea of life without compass or guide?
V. 61, p. 181

If any man desires to act according to the mind of God, light will come to him sooner or later.
V. 47, p. 27

No man, who acts honestly up to the light he has, will be left in the dark.
V. 61, p. 114

If the price at which you shall have a true experience is that of sorrow, buy the truth at that price.
V. 61, p. 114

Let us set our heart upon this, that we mean to have, by God's help, all that the infinite goodness of God is ready to bestow.
V. 28, p. 303

Expect that, if God has promised you anything, he will be true to his word; but, beyond that, do not expect anything beneath the moon.
V. 50, p. 356

Men are never right by accident, nor obedient to the Lord by chance; preparation of the heart is needed, and this the Lord must give.
V. 36, p. 308

SATAN

Satan will direct his engines against that very virtue for which you are most famous.
V. 11, p. 603

I have taken it as a certain sign that I am doing little good when the devil is quiet.
V. 11, p. 608

It is a great thing that a poor creature like you can actually vex the great prince of darkness and win his hate.
V. 11, p. 611

Satan's craft is deep to us, but it is very shallow to the Lord, whose wisdom goes far deeper than the cunning of the prince of darkness.
V. 24, p. 269

The victory of the devil in Eden is blotted out by the victory of Jesus at Calvary.
V. 36, p. 524

The devil greatly rejoices, because so many ministers do not preach the gospel: he is glad if he can poison the stream at the fountain–head.
V. 36, p. 424

If the devil can keep you from thinking, he will keep you from believing.
V. 36, p. 425

SCIENCE
❦

The doctrine we teach neither assails human science, nor fears it, nor flatters it, nor asks its aid.
V. 18, p. 472

The sacred art and mystery of believing in Jesus is the highest and noblest of all the practical sciences.
V. 57, p. 270

Science is notorious for being most scientific in the destruction of all the science that has gone before it.
V. 37, p. 46-47

Theories vaunted today will be scorned tomorrow.
V. 34, p. 153

The scientific jargon which makes God into an insensible force is covert atheism.
V. 35, p. 665

SCRIPTURE
❦

The Book grows upon you; as you dive into its depths you have a growing perception of the infinity which remains unexplored.
V. 33, p. 350

If science contradicts the Scripture so much the worse for science; the Scripture is true, whatever the theories of men may be.
V. 39, p. 475

Where sometimes different parts of Scripture seem to conflict with one another we should leave the explanation to the great Interpreter who alone can make all plain.
V. 53, p. 543

John Calvin, next to the apostle Paul, propounded truth more clearly than any other man that ever breathed.
V. 10, p. 310

If I could comprehend the whole of revelation I could scarcely believe it to be divine; I thank and bless God that he has designed to display before me a revelation far exceeding my poor limited abilities.
V. 12, p. 231-232

It is infinitely better to believe God's word than to interpret it.
V. 23, p. 30

How shall God be comprehensible by finite creatures, or his glorious truth be seen in all points by such poor mortals as we are.
V. 23, p. 30

When a man once gets to feed upon the Word of God, the rest is bones, and he lets the dogs have them.
V. 41, p. 439

Childlike confidence in the Word of God is the biggest form of common sense.
V. 31, p. 173

The worst forms of depression are cured when Holy Scripture is believed.
V. 35, p. 260

Personally, when I have been in trouble, I have read the Bible until a text has seemed to stand out of the Book and salute me, saying, "I was written specially for you."
V. 35, p. 261

The fact is you never were high, but the word of God was up with you; and you never were low but that the Scripture was down with you;
V. 35, p. 261

Rest assured that you never will be in a labyrinth so complicated that this Book, blessed of the Spirit, will not help you through.
V. 35, p. 262

It is always better where the word of God is silent to be silent ourselves.
V. 26, p. 68

Human thought is not the arbiter of truth, but the infallible Word is the end of all strife.
V. 25, p. 269

There is still an open Bible in our land and other lands and so long as that is the case we need not fear that Protestantism will die out.
V. 55, p. 558

The man who rejects the inspiration of the Word of God has given up the very foundation of faith.
V. 55, p. 243

Take this Book, and distill it into one word, and I will tell you what it is—it is Jesus.
V. 60, p. 232

All the doctrines of the Bible have a tendency, when properly understood and received, to foster the Christian's joy.
V. 60, p. 232

I would rather see the whole stock of my sermons in a blaze, all burned to ashes, than that they should keep anybody from reading the Bible.
V. 60, p. 237

Many religious books are a sort of mixture; their human thinking dilutes divine revelation.
V. 60, p. 238

The Word of God carries its own keys for all its locks; Scripture explains Scripture.
V. 36, p. 495

The word of God knows more about us than we can ever discover about ourselves.
V. 36, p. 89

Some seek the wisdom of man's thoughts rather than the wisdom of God's thoughts.
V. 31, p. 435

Judge everything that we say or that anyone else says by the supreme test of the Inspired Word.
V. 43, p. 426

If I say anything to you merely on my own authority, reject it; but if it be on the authority of the word of God, reject it at your peril.
V. 43, p. 426

Always be sure that those who would make you think lightly of the Scriptures are leading you away with the error of the wicked.
V. 43, p. 428

The Holy Spirit puts into the Word a power which makes it go right into your heart with the very tone and majesty of the God of Grace.
V. 44, p. 317

The worst weapon you can use is the Bible; it is intended for us to live upon—not to be the weapon of our controversies.
V. 44, p. 319

The Word of God shall endure forever and triumph over the ruin of all the words of men.
V. 18, p. 50

God's words are never to be taken at a discount, but with such blessed interest as your faith is able to apply thereto.
V. 12, p. 656

Is God's word only true when finite reason approves it?
V. 18, p. 476

SECOND COMING
℘

God will never suffer this world, which has once seen Christ's blood shed upon it, to be always the devil's stronghold.
M. & E., p. 719

We are not discouraged by the length of his delays; or the long period which he allots to the church in which to struggle with little success and much defeat.
M. & E., p. 719

We may desire the coming of the Lord, but we ought also to be in sympathy with the delay of the Most High, to which his loving heart inclines him.
V. 19, p. 438

One reason why I think the world's present state will not wind up for the present is, because all the prophets say it will.
V. 11, p. 273

When all mankind shall behold the Son of Man on the clouds of heaven, what conviction shall seize every mind! there will be no agnostics then!
V. 29, p. 132

There is a people who love him, a secret people who cling to him, and when he comes, as come he must ere long, they will welcome him and partake of his glory.
V. 31, p. 324

What astonishment will seize the sons of men when they see the King in His Glory, whom they would not understand nor serve when he came in the meekness and gentleness of love.
V. 60, p. 88

When the Son of Man comes will he find many who can believe in a delaying God, and plead a long-dated promise waiting but never wearying?
V. 33, p. 282

It should be to us not only a prophesy assuredly believe, but a scene pictured in our souls and anticipated in our hearts.
V. 32, p. 592

His manifestation will be our manifestation, and the day in which he is revealed in glory then shall his saints be glorified with him.
V. 25, p. 313

At the Lord's supper, there is no drinking into his cup to its fullness, unless you hear him say, "Until I come."
V. 33, p. 592

They will not be able to lift a finger against him when he comes to judge the living and the dead.
V. 14, p. 240

We have heard that Christ is coming and there is pressing need for someone to come, for this poor old machine of a world creaks dreadfully.
V. 14, p. 155

SELF–DENIAL
❦

Jesus asks us to give up nothing that is really for our good.
V. 61, p. 381

Jesus Christ asks us only for such self–denial as shall promote our everlasting welfare.
V. 61, p. 381

Selfishness is as foreign to Christianity as darkness is to light.
V. 18, p. 23

The hardest self–denial is to get away from all confidence in your own doings and feelings, and everything that comes of yourself.
V. 41, p. 75

We must either deny ourselves, or we shall deny our Lord; if we cleave to self-confidence we shall not cleave to him.
V. 34, p. 397

SELF–ESTEEM
❦

If any man will not acknowledge that he is desperately inclined to self–esteem, his denial of this truth is the best proof of it.
V. 3, p. 393

The more high in grace the more low in self–esteem.
V. 59, p. 125

It is not being better in your own esteem, it is being utterly
undone in your own esteem, which makes you ready for Christ.
V. 16, p. 348

Many are not really living so near to God as they think they
are; it is easy to frequent Bible classes and conferences and
excited public meetings and to fill oneself with the gas of
self–esteem.
V. 19, p. 308

I am always afraid of people who are so very good in their
own esteem; superfine, hot pressed perfectionism is generally
very poor stuff.
V. 42, p. 499

Always lowly should we be in our own esteem for he that
thinks himself to be something when he is nothing deceives
himself. (Gal. 6:3)
V. 13, p. 242

Few can bear to be surrounded with an atmosphere of esteem
without beginning to esteem themselves much too highly.
V. 36, p. 469

As we get weighed down with mercy we shall begin to sink in
our own esteem.
V. 44, p. 485

He that is down need fear no fall but he that rises very high
in his own esteem is not far from destruction.
V. 44, p. 489

There is that abominable pit of selfishness and self–esteem
and pride and self–seeking into which our feet so easily glide:
we are always something when Christ is nothing; we are
always nothing when Christ is all–in–all to us.
V. 19, p. 260

As a child of God grows in sanctification he deepens in humility, and as he advances to perfection he sinks in his own self–esteem.

V. 30, p. 627

Such is the power of self–esteem that though sin abounds in the sinner he will not readily be brought to feel or confess its existence.

V. 19, p. 73

The more our self–esteem increases the more firmly do we fasten the door against Christ.

V. 53, p. 160

The straight gate is not wide enough to allow that man to enter who is great in his own esteem.

V. 5, p. 375

Ruth had little self-esteem, and therefore she won the esteem of others.

V. 31, p. 401

Self–esteem is a moth which wears away the garments of virtue.

V. 19, p. 309

Anything is better than vain glory and self–esteem.

V. 26, p. 269

Some knowledge puffs up but knowledge of Christ makes us humble and the more we have of it the less we are in our own esteem.

V. 23, p. 319

I know that an accurate estimate of my own heart can never do otherwise than lower my self–esteem.

V. 55, p. 378

The sweet apples of self–esteem are a deadly poison, who would wish to be destroyed thereby?

V. 55, p. 378

Men akin to Jesus live for God and their fellowmen, unostentatious because of their failures, unselfish because self is held in low esteem.
V. 55, p. 382

If we had more faith we should sink in our own esteem, but we should greatly rise in our influence upon others.
V. 55, p. 242

Every worker will, in proportion as the desire for God's glory shall increase, feel himself to be less and less and still less in his own esteem.
V. 51, p. 79

Whenever you get one inch above the ground in your own esteem, you are one inch too high.
V. 41, p. 20

I do pray that you and I may be taught of God until we grow less and less, and come to be nothing at all in our own esteem.
V. 45, p. 45

Low thoughts of self should always be associated with high thoughts of Christ; for they are both products of the Spirit of God.
V. 36, p. 470

He that has high thoughts of himself is not necessarily a man of a clean life.
V. 36, p. 471

He that feels himself to be unworthy has something about him that God esteems.
V. 36, p. 471

If you have no confidence in yourself, your soul is one great vacuum and you can hold the more of Christ.
V. 36, p. 478

Why does the Lord declare the conversion of those who were out of the way? I think it is to destroy pride and self–esteem.
V. 32, p. 503

In proportion as a man grows in grace he decreases in his own esteem, and his brethren increase in his estimation.
V. 32, p. 110

How can we see God while our eyes are blinded with self?
V. 32, p. 435

How can that be a perfect character which finds its basis in self–esteem?
V. 25, p. 315

SELF EXAMINATION

He that cannot bear examination will have to bear condemnation.
V. 61, p. 112

He that dare not search himself will find that God will search him.
V. 61, p. 112

Every man ought to try to know all he can about himself.
V. 42, p. 100

If you cannot instruct your own heart, and drill a truth into your own soul, you do not know how to teach other people.
V. 42, p. 135

SELF–RIGHTEOUSNESS

Self–righteousness is sometimes a delusion, but it generally begins by a man's attempt to delude himself.
V. 45, p. 282

If you come to the place of supposing that you are the only man left who holds sound doctrine, you will become a bigot.
V. 47, p. 73

You were never drunkards and yet you will perish with the drunkards unless you repent and trust in Jesus.
V. 41, p. 78

SELFISHNESS
℘

If you would seek happiness, seek it at the expense of your selfishness; cut up your selfishness and you will be happy.
V. 2, p. 880

If to serve the Lord be not enough reward, let those who look for more go their selfish way: if heaven be not enough, let those who despise it seek their heaven below.
V. 18, p. 427

Where our selfishness and our self will come in, there our sorrows begin.
V. 47, p. 378

Self–confidence is the death of confidence in God; reliance upon talent, tact, experience, and thing of that kind, kills faith.
V. 34, p. 340

Selfishness is sordid, and, like the serpent, has dust appointed to be its meat.
V. 22, p. 419

No man ever sets a high price upon self and Christ at the same time.
V. 22, p. 8

You can always find reasons, such as they are, when you want to pursue a career of self-indulgence.
V. 35, p. 582

The most unreasonable reasons will come cropping up if you want to do what your flesh desires.
V. 35, p. 582

The more self sinks, the more Christ rises: like the two scales of a balance; one must go down that the other may go up: self must sink in repentance that Christ may rise by faith.
V. 35, p. 130

We are in danger of losing our respect for our fellows if we think so much of ourselves.
V. 55, p. 463

Self–sufficiency is inefficiency: the fullness of self is a double emptiness.
V. 29, p. 424

SEPARATION
❧

The path of separation may be the path of sorrow, but it is the path of safety.
V. 10, p. 375

To try to be a worldly Christian or a Christian worldling is an impossible thing.
V. 14, p. 665

The very essence of the Christian faith is separation from the world.
V. 14, p. 665

SERVICE
❧

The first thing for our own usefulness, is to keep ourselves in perpetual communion with the Lord Jesus.
M. & E., p. 49

Bad nurture in their spiritual infancy often causes converts to fall into a despondency from which they never recover.
M. & E., p. 296

To war against Him is madness, to serve him is glory.
M. & E., p. 413

The kind of service which seems most commonplace among men is often the most precious unto God.
V. 37, p. 320

Beware of having so much to do that you really do nothing at all because you do not wait upon God for the power to do it right.
V. 49, p. 464

Use the means but when you have done all, trust in God as though you had done nothing.
V. 21, p. 74

Do not be affected in your piety, as if you were going to walk to heaven on stilts: walk on your own feet and if you have a grand work to do, do it with genuine simplicity which is next akin to sublimnity.
V. 26, p. 495

Joseph and Nicodemus both illustrate the dreadful truth that it is hard for them that have riches to enter into the kingdom of God; but they also show us that when they do enter they frequently excel.
V. 24, p. 163

If you could restrict the Christian from the service of God, you would debar him from his highest joy.
V. 15, p. 454

The great destroyer of good works is the ambition to do great works.
V. 21, p. 5

The Lord first gives good works and then in his grace rewards us for them.
V. 21, p. 119

No life can surpass that of a man who quietly continues to serve God in the place where providence has placed him.
V. 22, p. 439

Circles are admired, not because of their largeness but because of their roundness, so you will have honour from God, not according to the size of your sphere but according to the completeness with which you fill it.
V. 59, p. 596

A nursery maid having the care of two or three children, teaching them the sweet story of the love of Christ, and seeking to bring their hearts to Jesus, may be more faithful than I am with a large congregation.

V. 59, p. 596

To save one soul is worthy of a life of service.

V. 59, p. 389

To attempt a difficulty may be laudable, but to rush upon an impossibility is madness.

V. 35, p. 446

We may be precious in the Lord's sight, although our schemes end in disappointment.

M. & E., p. 26

I wish the whole church of Christ would realize that her greatest victories have usually been accomplished by those who did not seem, from the human standpoint, competent for the task.

V. 55, p. 559

Heads are won by reasoning, but hearts are won by witness–bearing.

V. 30, p. 197

Argument which appeals only to the intellect is poor fuel with which to kindle the fire of love to Christ.

V. 30, p. 197

When you can sing with the psalmist, "My cup runneth over," mind you that you call somebody to come and catch the spillings.

V. 47, p. 378

It is an instinct of the Christian life to wish to be doing something to glorify God and to save the souls of others.

V. 36, p. 510

Are we to be so looking after the sheep as never to do honour to the Shepherd?

V. 36, p. 59

The service of the world is much sterner and more exacting much more wearisome, than the service of our Lord Jesus Christ.
V. 32, p. 16

Whenever God designs to make his servants eminently useful, he lets them know their frailty.
V. 24, p. 596

If sitting at the feet of Jesus be regarded as of secondary importance then both strength and will to serve the Lord will decline.
V. 16, p. 232

To labour for Christ is a pleasant thing, but beware of doing it mechanically; and this you can only prevent by diligently cultivating personal communion with Christ.
V. 16, p. 234

Holy service in constant fellowship with God is heaven below.
V. 33, p. 274

Serve your Lord with an intensity which others cannot reach and live for him with an ardour of which they cannot conceive.
V. 18, p. 18

Those feeble efforts of yours which were so imperfect that you could scarcely hope them to be successful, are all cooperating to produce a victory the shouts of which shall be heard all down the ages.
V. 14, p. 237

Christian service is the spontaneous outburst of indwelling grace, and though it may be toil to the lip and toil to the brain, it is perfect rest to the spirit.
V. 15, p. 221

To trust in the means without God, is presumption; and to profess to trust in God without the means is only another form of presumption.
V. 44, p. 110

Husbandman your great Employer sent you out to sow the seed, but if no grain of it should ever come up, after you have sowed as he told you, he will never lay the blame of a defective harvest to you.

V. 8, p. 22

SIN

If the Saviour has not given you a hatred for sin and a love of holiness, He has done nothing in you of a saving character.

M. & E., p. 79

I find in God all that I want; but I find in myself nothing but sin and misery.

M. & E., p. 114

Do you give fair names to foul sins? call them what you will, they will smell no sweeter.

M. & E., p. 197

Grace is at a low ebb in that soul which can even raise the question of how far it may go in worldly conformity.

M. & E., p. 341

Amid the cheerfulness of household gatherings it is easy to slide into sinful levites, and to forget our avowed character as Christian.

M. & E., p. 721

The roots of sin run through and through our nature and grasp it with wonderful force, and keep up their grasp with marvelous tenacity.

V. 34, p. 473

Careless sinners talk about the hardness of God in condemning man to punishment, but once let the Holy Spirit show man the exceeding sinfulness of sin, and you will never hear a word about that.

V. 8, p. 267

When a sin does easily beset you, you must master your whole force and cry unto heaven for strength to overcome it.

V. 12, p. 534

One sin harboured in the soul will ruin you.
V. 12, p. 534

An unpardoned sinner sins cheaply compared with one of
God's own elect ones who has had communion with Christ.
V. 13, p. 245

Though no man is free from the commission of sin, yet every
converted man is free from the love of sin.
V. 35, p. 125

When a man has his face toward Jesus his back is necessarily
turned on his sins.
V. 21, p. 123

Is it not a sad proof of the alienation of our nature that
though God is everywhere we have to school ourselves to
perceive him anywhere?
V. 22, p. 411

I can understand your sinning, but I cannot understand your
finding pleasure in it if you are a true Christian.
V. 22, p. 416

The same sun which melts wax hardens clay; and the same
gospel which melts persons to repentance hardens others in
their sins.
V. 46, p. 271

There is a little hell within the heart of every child of God, and
only the great God of heaven can master that indwelling sin.
V. 18, p. 414

The deceivableness of sin is very great so that it adorns itself
with the colours of righteousness and makes men believe they
are pleasing God when they are offending him.
V. 19, p. 74

Man is so diseased [by sin] that he fancies disease to be
health, and judges healthy men to be under wild delusion.
V. 19, p. 75

Sin is worse than the devil, since it made the devil what he is.
V. 19, p. 77

The worldling says he wants to see life and therefore plunges into sin; fool that he is, he peers into the sepulcher to discover immortality.
V. 13, p. 646

The fact is, we are guilty, and we deserve the punishment which God apportions to guilt, and we must agree with that truth, grim as it looks, or else we cannot be friends with God.
V. 25, p. 63

Sin bribes the judgment, intoxicates the will and perverts the memory.
V. 27, p. 26

If I were to cry "fire, fire!" in this place tonight most of you would rush to the nearest exit; but when we tell you of what is infinitely worse–namely, of the wrath to come and the anger of Almighty God, you are in no great alarm.
V. 27, p. 28

Satan suggests to the heart, "If you had not sinned so much you might have been forgiven, but you have piled on the last ounce that has broken the back of mercy."
V. 27, p. 29

Expense, pain, disgrace, disease, poverty and an early death— all these are demanded by the drink demon, and his victims cheerfully pay the tax.
V. 27, p. 30

One sin will often kill another sin, as the miser shuns profligacy because he is too stingy to spend his money riotously.
V. 31, p. 665

If it had not been for the grace of God our sins would have shut us up in hell already, and even now they seek to drag us there.
V. 18, p. 365

A Christian man cannot indulge a known sin and yet walk with God.
V. 18, p. 365

As soon as we tolerate sin within ourselves, we lose power in prayer.
V. 18, p. 365

By the blood of Jesus you are under bonds to hate evil.
V. 18, p. 369

A child of God may, for awhile, be the captive of sin, but never a lover of sin.
V. 18, p. 369

When the Spirit of God makes a man see sin in its naked deformity, he is horrified.
V. 29, p. 127

Some preachers make out sin to be only a trifle, but God's word does not.
V. 54, p. 259

A man may sin and be saved but he cannot love sin and be saved.
V. 61, p. 114

A reprobate, after making a profession, may, perhaps, go back (to sin) and be comfortable, but a Christian never can.
V. 61, p. 164

Tell me that you are happy in your sin, and I tell you at once that you are dead in sin.
V. 61, p. 165

There is no sin that we cannot pray down and weep down if we live at the foot of the cross.
V. 60, p. 113

Sorrow for sin is sweet sorrow it is part of the Christian's experience which helps to fill his joy.
V. 60, p. 234

There is a mourning which comes from the Spirit of God; that is a joyful mourning, if I may use such a strange expression.
V. 60, p. 234

I never saw sin till that hour, when I saw it tear Christ's glories form his head; when it seemed for a moment even to withdraw the lovingkindness of God from him
V. 46, p. 4

Sin did condemn him; and inasmuch as sin condemned him, sin cannot condemn us,
V. 46, p. 7

He takes away form you that dagger of sin that is nestling in your bosom to destroy you.
V. 61, p. 381

If we tolerate the least sin, it is a burning drop in the veins of the soul.
V. 36, p. 520

Those engaged in evil designs have no other way of going than with tricks, devices, concealments, double meanings.
V. 36, p. 523

When men deny the Scriptures and the truth of God, they always go to work in an underhanded, mean, and serpentine style.
V. 36, p. 528

Do you cry out for what is called "liberty," that is licentiousness and permission to indulge your own passions?
V. 36, p. 528

A sinner's eye is never ready to see the Saviour till first he has seen the sin.
V. 28, p. 503

Depend upon it, that sin which you would save from slaughter will slaughter you.
V. 28, p. 646

All the prayers of godly men cannot alter the nature of sin.
V. 28, p. 178

Sin is fire, and it must burn, it is hell and it must torment the man who continues in it.
V. 28, p. 179

He took Eve out of the side of Adam when Adam slumbered, but he will not take sin out of you when you are asleep.
V. 32, p. 84

The wages of sin are full of travail and disappointment and anguish.
V. 32, p. 16

The loving God, compelled by love itself, frowns at sin.
V. 24, p. 62

Count it to be one of the most fearful curses that can happen to you to be happy in your sins.
V. 24, p. 65

Though all have sinned, and deserve the wrath of God, all unconverted men are not precisely in the same condition of mind in reference to the gospel.
V. 16, p. 157

Although in every case the carnal mind is enmity against God, yet there are influences at work which in many cases have mitigated, if not subdued that enmity.
V. 16, p. 157

I believe there are many persons who have been mercifully restrained from the grosser vices and exhibit everything that is pure and excellent in moral character.
V. 16, p. 158

Sin has polluted all our blood, and left the leprosy still in our veins as a legacy of ill to the last generation.
V. 15, p. 637

Never has the world seen another tyrant comparable to this.
V. 15, p. 637

In the holiest of men there is enough sin to destroy them if it were not for the grace of God.
V. 15, p. 642

Only in salvation from sin is there salvation from wrath.
V. 15, p. 639

The reason why sinners are not persuaded, in ninety-nine cases out of a hundred, is their love of sin.
V. 15, p. 285

The vilest sin is rampant–sin of which we dare not speak, it is so vile.
V. 42, p. 101

If sin had not madden men they would listen eagerly to every Word of God.
V. 25, p. 443

If you do not hate your sin, you will hate the gospel.
V. 62, p. 171

If sermons never aim at breaking your heart, do not waste any more Sundays in hearing them, for they are not God's Word.
V. 62, p. 173

Blindness of heart is not only a sin, it is also the punishment of sin.
V. 39, p. 188

Our sins must be abandoned, or we cannot receive a Saviour.
V. 12, p. 659

A little sin is like a small dose of a very potent poison: it is sufficient to destroy our peace and comfort.
V. 12, p. 354

Evil practice will drown the best of preaching.
V. 11, p. 494

Shall we not feel within our hearts a burning indignation against sin, because it is committed against so holy, so good, so glorious a being as the infinitely–blessed God?
V. 41, p. 304

If God had pardoned sin without atonement, he would have sat in the serene majesty of heaven, and we would have thought that sin was a trifling thing altogether beneath his notice.
V. 41, p. 7

So great is the ruin which sin has brought upon us, that it is truly indescribable.

V. 43, p. 434

Sin is a more horrible thing than imagination itself can conceive it to be.

V. 44, p. 331

There is a mysterious efficacy in the blood of Christ not only to make satisfaction for sin but also to work the death of sin.

V. 8, p. 95

The Scriptures cease to be sweet to us when sin becomes pleasant.

V. 18, p. 365

Services of the sanctuary are dull and lifeless when the heart is fascinated by evil.

V. 18, p. 365

Sin drives men mad: against their reason, against their own best interests, they follow after that which they know will destroy them.

V. 27, p. 27

The sin (of Sodom and Gomorrah) itself is infinitely worse than the fire which burned it up.

V. 58, p. 413

SINGING

Singing is the best thing to purge ourselves of evil thoughts.
V. 44, p. 106

At no time does God love his children's singing so well as when he has hidden his face from them.
V. 44, p. 106

That is true faith that can make them sing praises when God does not appear to them.
V. 44, p. 106

Sing then Christian, for singing pleases God.
V. 44, p. 106

SLANDER

I believe that, if there is anything you want to have well done, you had better do it yourself; but there is one exception to that rule and that is the matter of defending yourself.
V. 50, p. 89

Go and do the right thing and be no longer anxious about it, but leave the result with God.
V. 50, p. 89

If anyone says to you, "O you are a Methodist," take the imputation kindly; it is a most respectable name, some of the grandest men that ever lived were Methodist.
V. 24, p. 64

SORROW

Sometimes we are told that if we really believed that our friends would rise again and that they are safe and happy even now, we could not weep: why not? Jesus did.
V. 35, p. 344

A Jesus who never wept could never wipe away my tears.
V. 35, p. 346

Never draw the inference from sorrow that the subject of it is not beloved of God: you might more safely reason in the opposite way.
V. 26, p. 39

Constantly looking within your own self instead of looking alone to Christ is enough to breed misery in any heart.
V. 27, p. 75

You will find it the path of wisdom, when you have a great joy, to be afraid; but when you have a great sorrow, then have a high anticipation of blessing.
V. 41, p. 438

SOVEREIGNTY OF GOD
❦

Sovereignty is absolute but it is never absurd; there is always a justifiable cause for everything God does in the Kingdom of Grace.
V. 37, p. 475

I will venture to say that the sovereignty of God is never exercised apart from his mercy.
V. 56, p. 293

To this day, men cannot bear that doctrine [God's sovereignty]; free will suits them very well, but free grace does not.
V. 47, p. 567

It often is the case that God takes his servants home just when they are most useful.
V. 51, p. 391

Did you ever sit down and think, "What will my wife do when I am gone?" You do not like to think of it, then do not think of it, for it is no business of yours.
V. 51, p. 392

The church lost Stephen, but she gained Saul, and that was a very good exchange.
V. 51, p. 392

Out of the ranks of Satan's army he can take the boldest champion of evil and lay upon him the charge to become a leader to the hosts of the living God.
V. 51, p. 393

They were eager to destroy Christ out of diabolical malice, and yet all the while they were the instruments of the death by which we are redeemed from destruction.
V. 34, p. 237

Let Jehovah do absolutely as he wills, for his will must be perfect justice, perfect goodness, perfect righteousness.
V. 44, p. 592

Have you been humbled in the dust to know that God has a right to do with you as he pleases?
V. 54, p. 252

God sometimes allows us to see the sins of others, to teach us to admire his sovereignty, which plucked us as brands from the burning.
V. 47, p. 252

In the infinite sovereignty of God he passed by the fallen angels, but he chose to raise fallen man.
V. 36, p. 519

The Lord in his gracious sovereignty meets with persons who have never sought him, and brings them to himself.
V. 32, p. 494

In the daylight of eternity we shall all admiringly discern that sovereignty was never dissociated from justice.
V. 14, p. 351

God condescends not to explain his modes of action, nor to prove his own justice, for who is he that he should stand at our bar.
V. 14, p. 350

There is the best of reasons why everything that Jesus does should please his people, because everything he does is right.
V. 41, p. 317

It is the bread that feeds, it is the medicine that heals; but it is God who works by these means; or if he pleases, he works without them.
V. 44, p. 315

The breath of your nostrils is so absolutely under God's control that all the physicians in the world could not extend the lease of your life.
V. 58, p. 17

The sovereignty of God is always exercised in such a way that the pure in heart may rejoice in it.
V. 26, p. 684

SUCCESS

We shall not be rewarded even according to our own success.
V. 37, p. 475

The godly housewife, in her cottage, with four or five children trained for God may be reckoned of God among the first; and the able speaker; in his pulpit, who has thousands hanging on his lips may be reckoned among the last.
V. 37, p. 475

He sent Jeremiah to weep over a nation to whom his tears brought no repentance and no reformation.
V. 37, p. 475

He sent Noah to preach for 120 years and never got a soul beside his own family into the ark.
V. 37, p. 475

Suppose that you are not only weak but that you are weakness itself,—that you are nothing and nobody; when you have reached that point, the cause of your weeping will have vanished, because where you end, there God begins.
V. 51, p. 188

Never imagine that you can be a loser by trusting in God.
V. 54, p. 92

TEMPTATION

It is better to be so well armed that the devil will not attract you, than to endure the perils of the fight, even though you come off a conqueror.
M. & E., p. 81

We are constantly opposed, and yet perpetually preserved.
M. & E., p. 97

There is nothing in this world to foster a Christian's piety, but everything to destroy it.
M. & E., p. 149

I think no man in such imminent danger as the man who thinks there is no danger.
V. 45, p. 2

We are tempted by our mercies and we are tempted by our miseries.
V. 45, p. 2

So ready are we to sin, that to prevail over one temptation is a great joy.
V. 31, p. 668

You may, in order to help yourself, do in five minutes what you cannot undo in fifty years.
V. 20, p. 30

You may bring upon yourself a life long series of trials by one single unbelieving action.
V. 20, p. 30

There are certain graces which are never produced in Christians, to a high degree, except by severe temptations.
V. 45, p. 207

I would like to get hold of that young man who has lately been listening to skeptical teachers, and whisper in his ear, "Cling to your faith, young man; for, in losing that you will lose all."
V. 45, p.213

Today Satan tempts ministers of Christ to soften down the gospel and adopt it to the age, and make it popular.
V. 36, p. 525

Satan will be wise enough to leave off tempting when he finds that the more he attempts to drive us, the more we go in the opposite direction.

V. 42, p. 142

If you deliberately incite another to sin by daring him to do it, or by any other method of tempting him to do wrong, you shall share the accusation at the last great day.

V. 41, p. 89

You and I encounter some temptations, but Christ endured them all.

V. 58, p. 31

Satan tempts many believers to run before the cloud to carve their own fortunes, to steer their own vessels, but mischief will befall all who yield to this temptation.

V. 9, p. 5

Christ the anointed one, the high priest of our confession, is in his complex character able to help them that are tempted.

V. 9, p. 10

TRIALS

No Christian has enjoyed perpetual prosperity; no believer can always keep his harp from the willows.

M. & E., p. 240

A tried Christian grows rich by his losses, he rises by his falls, he lives by dying, and becomes full by being emptied.

M. & E., p. 279

The idea of strangeness in our trials must be banished at once and forever, for the Head of all saints knows by experience the grief which we think is peculiar.

M. & E., p. 304

It is true that we endure trials, but it is also true that we are delivered out of them.

M. & E., p. 322

Better a brief warfare and eternal rest, than false peace and everlasting torment.
M. & E., p. 727

What may seem defeat for us may be victory to him.
M. & E., p. 717

The height of affliction is as much under the Lord's control as the bright summer days when all is bliss.
M. & E., p. 717

If you are right before the Lord, through faith in Christ, your enemies cannot make you wrong by anything they say.
V. 18, p. 115

Elijah may call down fire from heaven to consume the sacrifice, but no fire from heaven can consume his trouble, he must endure it.
V. 57, p. 398

A man may be a true believer and yet feel he is sinking fast into the mire and clay of unbelief as some of us know to our own lamentation and dismay.
V. 11, p. 291

Do you know that affliction is a covenant blessing? therefore no argument derived from circumstances is worth listening to.
V. 19, p. 689

God comes into our heart–he finds it full–he begins to break our comforts and make it empty; then there is more room for grace.
M. & E., p. 86

Fret not over your heavy troubles, for they are heralds of weighty mercies.
M. & E., p. 86

Many a man of God has lived through a hundred troubles when he thought one would kill him.
V. 35, p. 430

The best child of God may be the greatest sufferer, and his suffering may appear to be crushing, killing and overwhelming.
V. 19, p. 14

Great trials are the clouds out of which God sends showers of great mercies.
V. 21, p. 74

God's children have often been ripened through sickness, they are like the sycamore fig which never gets sweet until it is bruised.
V. 34, p. 60

A rebellious heart comes out of affliction worse rather than better.
V. 29, p. 427

We are the better for the fire, the anvil, and the hammer with which our enemies have been good enough to work upon us.
V. 34, p. 584

More closeness to God, more confidence in him and more joy in him often comes to the child of God when he is most under fire.
V. 34, p. 584

In years gone by every form and fashion of abuse was heaped upon me and what a wonderful advertisement it was, what kindness they were doing to me without intending it.
V. 39, p. 150

Marah is, after all, more noteworthy than Elim; and truly, there does come to God's people something better out of their troubles than their joys.
V. 39, p. 146

If ever God honors one of his children in public, I bear witness that he has a way of flogging him behind the door, to make him feel that he has nothing wherein to glory save only in the Lord.
V. 46, p. 483

To go to heaven is not such an easy matter that every fool may do it before breakfast.
V. 47, p. 378

What is needed is not the removal of the trouble but the conquest of self.
V. 47, p. 378

Your heart is breaking, you say, because of your troubles, but it needs more breaking; for if it was broken, the trouble would not brake it.
V. 35, p. 430

If God sends six troubles, they are six times better than one though they seem to be six times worse.
V. 23, p. 31

Two or three times in almost every year I have to hear the Lord preach to me in the chamber of sickness and I am unable to preach to you.
V. 35, p. 118

I praise the Lord for raising me up [from sickness] again and again and renewing my strength.
V. 35, p. 118

Oh, the great goodness of a great God to great sinners, in times of their great need.
V. 35, p. 117

All the dogs of affliction are muzzled until God sets them free.
V. 35, p. 429

If He wills that we bear a certain weight, no one can add half an ounce more.
V. 35, p. 427

Because you are bound for heaven you will meet with storms on your voyage to glory.
V. 35, p. 430

The worst evils of life are those which do not exist except in our imagination.
T. D., V. 1, p. 401

If we had no troubles but real troubles, we should not have a tenth of our present sorrow.
T. D., V. 1, p. 401

It is never said, "whom the Lord loves he enriches" but it is said, "whom the Lord loves he chastens."
V. 26, p. 39

Beneath the great flood tides of outward affliction our Lord felt an undercurrent of joy.
V. 26, p. 674

It is better to smart until one is black and blue under the rod of God than to be set on a high throne by the world or the devil.
V. 25, p. 71

Even the wickedness of man, by driving us nearer to God, should prove a motive–power to produce more exemplary lives.
V. 31, p. 156

That same process, which in gracious souls, has brought forth everything that is pure and lovely, has in others produced everything that is malicious and envious.
V. 27, p. 638

Meditation is as silver; but tribulation is as fine gold.
V. 37, p. 140

Some virtues cannot be produced in us without affliction.
V. 27, p. 640

There is a very sweet grace called sympathy which is seldom found in persons who have had no troubles.
V. 27, p. 641

Let us go forth, not to ask for affliction, that would be unwise, but to accept it hopefully when it comes.
V. 27, p. 644

I find it a blessed thing in life when troubles with all these difficult problems to fall back upon God who will overrule it all.
V. 41, p. 30

God leads us into the wilderness and leaves us there just to prove we are not the rich and great and believing people we thought we were.
V. 40, p. 45

To suffer dishonor for Christ is honour and to suffer shame for him is the very top of all glory.
V. 30, p. 383

Do you know what it is to be in such pain that you could not bear one more turn of the screw, and then in faintness fall back upon your pillow and feel that even then you could not be more happy unless you were caught up to heaven.
V. 37, p. 42

Everything that will abide the fire must go through the fire, that it may be both proved and improved.
V. 37, p. 493

I would sooner feel God's hand heavy upon me than to be forsaken of him.
V. 37, p. 494

No man has ever been able to find a perfectly smooth path through this mortal life.
V. 27, p. 149

A man who has never had any trouble is very awkward when he tries to comfort troubled hearts.
V. 45, p. 452

Some of us can say of affliction, "You have done us more good than all our joys put together."
V. 45, p. 453

There is no man who is so ready to cope with the troubles of life as the one who knows that all is right for eternity.
V. 45, p. 284

Trials make a man see whether he really is all that he thinks he is.
V. 47, p. 178

You may not say, because you are certain that the Lord loves you, that therefore he will not allow you to be tried, because that is clearly contrary to Scripture.
V. 47, p. 171

The Lord does often take his children into the stripping room and into the starving room and let them see that all their afflictions are less than they deserve.
V. 47, p. 40

I have lost a great many on whose fidelity I thought I could depend; but since I depend on the Lord all the more, I am a gainer by ungrateful desertions.
V. 36, p. 515

It is a happy day for a man when he knows in whose hand is the rod, and he learns to trace his troubles to God.
V. 24, p. 63

He has ordained our trials for judgment, and established them for correction.
V. 24, p. 63

If there be a trial in the Christian life, Christ has borne it, and Christ is with us, bearing it still.
V. 18, p. 54

He who rejects the yoke of Christ, bows his neck to something worse by far.
V. 18, p. 60

You pray against promotion when you pray against affliction.
V. 33, p. 513

The Lord has exempted you from the curse, but he has not exempted you from the chastisement.
V. 14, p. 684

Every time of want, every time of pain, every time of depression, is but the commencement of a season of blessing.
V. 42, p. 608

Worse difficulties have occurred to us than any that have ever been penned by the most notorious infidels.
V. 32, p. 435

Let every pain, let every weakness, let every sorrow, let every sin, drive you to God.
V. 60, p. 248

You may abound in prayer, and in thanksgiving and in patience, and yet, for all that, all God's waves and billows may roll over you and you may be brought into the depths of soul–trouble.
V. 47, p. 172

When the Lord pulls a man down, he does it in order that he may build him up again: when he breaks a man's heart, it is not for the mere breaking's sake, it is that he may make it anew.
V. 47, p. 47

If you speculate and lose your prosperity, do not say you are losing all for Christ's sake; call it the fruit of your own folly.
V. 10, p. 5

Contention with inbred lusts, denial of proud self, resistance to sin, all are forms of suffering with Christ.
V. 10, p. 8

The burden of life is heavy, my sister, then do not try to carry it, but cast your burden upon the Lord.
V. 50, p. 355

When the children of God become exceedingly faint and feeble, and their sense of impurity and nothingness becomes painful and even killing to them, the Lord has ways of restoring and reviving their spirits.
V. 18, p. 6

One Christian man said, "I used to have many disappointments until I changed one letter of the word, and chopped it into two, so that instead of disappointments, I read it "his appointments."
V. 41, p. 321

If men despise you, it matters little when God has blessed you.
V. 38, p. 18

It is hopeful when we find that all our ills lie within the ring–fence of omnipotent over-ruling.
V. 38, p. 5

If we had the choice of our crosses, the one we should choose would turn out to be more inconvenient than that which God appoints for us.
V. 38, p. 5

When the Lord smites you with his left hand, he sustains you with his right hand.
V. 38, p. 6

Tried Christians see how God sustains in trouble, and how he delivers them out of it.
V. 38, p. 11

"All things work together for good to them that love God" and chastisement is chief among those "all things."
V. 38, p. 9

Let us count it to be our highest gain to suffer loss for him.
V. 12, p. 651

There is a difference between chastening and punishment; every one can see the distinction between the chastening of a father and the punishment of a judge.
V. 12, p. 655

Blessed be God that this present state is not an eternity.
V. 13, p 431

We have almost courted suffering itself by reason of the richness of the consolation which suffering times have always brought with them.
V. 42, p. 163

When your grief presses you to the very dust, worship there.
V. 42, p. 134

Solomon in all his glory was not arrayed so gloriously as poor Job.
V. 12, p. 354

How often God has thrown a man on a sick bed to make him well.
V. 11, p. 595

You shall be more happy that everything should disappoint you than that everything should please you, if it be God's will.
V. 42, p. 116

Depend upon it, there is no way of bringing affliction upon ourselves like refusing to bear affliction.
V. 42, p. 365

If we will not take up the cross, the cross may take us up; and that is a far worse lot than the other.
V. 42, p. 365

To give him the highest praise when you are in the deepest waters, this is acceptable with him.
V. 61, p. 218

How despicable our troubles and trials appear when we look back upon them; but when we get to heaven they will seem to us just nothing at all.
V. 44, p. 104

Underneath each trouble there is a faithful purpose and a kind intent.
V. 24, p. 269

Holy men must expect to be misrepresented, misinterpreted, and often maligned, while hypocrites have their reward in undeserved homage.
V. 58, p. 27

Men have written out your death-warrant; but the Lord Jesus has not signed it, and therefore it cannot be executed.
V. 36, p. 484

A man with God may be afflicted with a hundred diseases at once, but he has the best of health, even the sanity of his soul.
V. 41, p. 30

TRINITY
⅗

God must give all, and Christ must be all, and the Spirit must
work all, and man must be as clay in the potter's hand.
V. 17, p. 382

TRUTH
⅗

I would not tell a lie to save a soul.
V. 7, p. 485

It is hard to tell where a boast ends and a lie begins for boasters have talked themselves into believing their own bombast.
Proverbs & Sayings, p. 4

By the everliving God there is truth somewhere, and that truth we
will find out if we can and having found it we will hold it fast.
V. 19, p. 105

He is the man whom the Lord accepts, who feels that if the
heavens fall it is not for him to prop them up with a lie if that
could make them stand.
V. 27, p. 113

A lie to our fellowmen is meanness, but a lie to God is madness.
V. 33, p. 402

He who seeks comfort at the expense of truth will be a fool
for his pains.
V. 35, p. 104

Truth of necessity is intolerant of falsehood.
V. 25, p. 275

In the power of the Holy Spirit truth is invincible.
V. 37, p. 50

If I could, by telling one lie, put out the flames of hell, I
would not do it.
V. 14, p. 331

No lie that was ever told was so incredible but what somebody or other was found to believe it.
V. 14, p. 429

Being sincere in believing a lie does not transform the lie into
the truth.
V. 61, p. 544

As long as there is false doctrine, there shall be a protest-
ing reformer.
V. 36, p. 525

You must honour your promise even if you feel ashamed of
the person to whom it was made.
V. 28, p. 299

Our testimony to the joy, peace, comfort and strength which
faith in Jesus brings ought to be accepted being corroborated
by the witness of thousands of men of unblemished character.
V. 15, p. 282

There is no room for indeference where the gospel is concerned; it is either the most astounding of impostures or the
most amazing of revelations.
V. 3, p. 697

Great must be the truth which forces itself upon the conviction of minds so dark and benighted as ours.
V. 13, p. 705

Self–evident truth will always find self–evident fools to
contradict it.
V. 18, p. 711

The strict literal truth in all things should be the law of the
child of God.
V. 18, p. 22

We want to know in our own soul what truth is—the truth
concerning sin so as to hate it—the truth concerning the
atonement so as to prize it—the truth concerning the Deity of
Christ so as to rejoice in it.
V. 43, p. 426

We believe in truth that never alters, and never can be altered, but stands immutable as God himself.
V. 43, p. 427

UNBELIEF
ᑍᑎ

The worst darkness is that which so blinds a man that he thinks he can see better than other people.
V. 30, p. 401

There is more infidelity in the best believer than he dreams of.
V. 33, p. 484

Some Christians talk about believing in God for eternity, but for this day and next week they are full of fear.
V. 33, p. 488

Let it be clearly known that some of us who can this day speak with fully assured confidence, have in days gone bye been sorely shaken.
V. 33, p. 545

What simpletons we are to fancy that if we do not see a way of deliverance, God does not see one either.
V. 33, p. 545

When you so believe a truth as to put it to bed and smother it with neglect, it is much the same as if you did not believe it at all.
V. 30, p. 494

He that made them a path through the deep waters could make a path for waters to come to them.
V. 39, p. 148

Doubts are dreary things in time of sorrow, like wasps they sting the soul.
M. & E., p. 224

Do we not often sit and fret together in most delightful misery and try to cheer each other downwards into greater depths of despair?
V. 42, p. 234

Certain individuals say that they will never believe what they cannot understand; if they adhere to that determination, they will never believe in their own existence, for they certainly cannot understand that.
V. 52, p. 122

Some of you are now daily hearing truth which has saved thousands, but it does not save you; you are hearing the very truth which peoples heaven, but yet it leaves you without hope of eternal life.
V. 23, p. 307

It cannot but grieve gracious souls to see what pains men take to go to hell.
M. & E., p. 615

When unregenerate men tell us that they cannot see the beauty of the gospel, we are not at all astonished—we never thought they could.
V. 26, p. 679

It is a very sad thing to think that many are living in total darkness next door to the light.
V. 10, p. 101

Many men indulge in iniquities of which they might be ashamed if they did not make a cloak of their atheism.
V. 41, p. 433

Numbers of people to this day, do not receive Christ because faith in him is not fashionable.
V. 40, p. 533

O simpletons, to lose your souls for the sake of a little worldly grandeur! God save us all from such insanity as that!
V. 40, p. 533

Isaiah was sublime in thought, attractive in word, and affectionate in spirit, and yet they did not believe his testimony.
V. 31, p. 315

It is a miracle of madness that men should be indifferent to the interest of their souls.
V. 14, p. 424

You could trust God, you say, in a storm at sea; but can you trust him about that bad debt on your books.
V. 46, p. 230

Most of us are scarcely aware of what an awful amount of skepticism still lures within our breast.
V. 46, p. 229

Beware of the unbelief which enables you to trifle; for trifling with eternal things is suicide of the soul.
V. 36, p. 306

If you refuse the bread of life, can we pity you if you die of hunger?
V. 36, p. 477

We are prone to unbelief, this noxious weed grows without sowing.
V. 28, p. 511

I may doubt myself; I may go further, I may despair of myself, but I must not doubt the Lord.
V. 18, p. 69

Doubting and unbelief are to be abhorred, and to be confessed with tears before God.
V. 18, p. 71

O unbelief, to what madness do you go, that even when men are driven to starvation, they will not turn to God.
V. 42, p. 142

Doubt is the death of all comfort, the destruction of all force, the enemy of God and man.
V. 38, p. 93

There is very little room for Christ in colleges and universities, very little room for him in the seats of learning.

V. 8, p. 704

UNITY
❦

Let us have large–heartedness and brotherly kindness—not keeping back our views but holding with a firm hand everything we have received from the Holy Spirit, and yet loving the whole household of faith.

V. 59, p. 142

We are to bear one another's burdens in respect to sympathy, but not in the sense of substitution.

V. 13, p. 639

Unity in error is unity in ruin.

V. 11, p. 11

VICTORY
❦

God often helps his servants to laugh at the very things which before seemed great burdens to them.

V. 46, p. 235

There has come to you a most substantial benefit from everything you are called upon to endure.

V. 46, p. 242

The great rumbling wagons of tribulation have been those which have brought the heaviest weight of treasure.

V. 46, p. 242-243

Job forgot his misery when, in a short time, he had double as much of all he possessed before.

V. 46, p. 243

Recollect that you are journeying to your Father's house, so be of good courage, for you shall forget your misery, and only remember it as waters that pass away.

V. 46, p. 244

By simple obedience to his will, and keeping the faith, and walking in his truth, I have been more than conqueror through him that loved me.

V. 25, p. 23

Rest assured that Christ's victory is ours, and he will no more forget us than a woman will cease to think of the son of her womb.

V. 14, p. 238

WISDOM

We do not all grow wiser as we grow older, but it ought to be so.

V. 20, p. 353

Do not imagine, as some do, that religion consists in a wild fanaticism which never considers, calculates, judges, estimates or ponders; for such an imagination will be the reverse of truth.

V. 23, p. 313

The wisdom which is true and real the Lord is prepared to give to those who confess their unwisdom.

V. 26, p. 678

The pomp, and power, and wisdom, and cunning of the world were not with Jesus, and he thanked God that he was not encumbered with such doubtful gain.

V. 26, p. 681

The history of philosophy is a record of the insanities of mankind: a catalogue of lunacies.

V. 26, p. 682

If great men, if eminent men, if so called learned men, are not converted, do not be cast down about it,—it is not likely they will be.

V. 26, p. 684

The passions, instead of being ruled by reason, often demand to hold the reigns.

V. 24, p. 76

Reason instead of being guided by God's Word, chooses to obey a depraved imagination and demands to become a separate power and to judge God himself.
V. 24, p. 76

Keep clear of the unbelieving advise of good people, and then you will have less to fear from the bad ones.
V. 18, p. 656

The first thing is not to have common sense and be wise, but to have a sense of God's presence, which is better than common sense.
V. 27, p. 90

As to his life as a whole Solomon perpetrated the greatest folly; the cream of wisdom when curdled makes the worst kind of folly.
V. 34, p. 594

Even if he has no other sense, he acts sensibly when he keeps quiet; he has at least sense enough to conceal his lack of it.
P. & Q.s p. 75

Have a judicious mind towards men and do not fall into credulity nor suspicion.
P. & Q.s 75, B. 45

He who lives in perpetual distrust of his fellow creatures cannot be happy; I would rather be too credulous towards them than too suspicious.
V. 53, p. 194

If human wisdom wins men's minds, what shall infallible wisdom do?
V. 23, p. 223

It is God's prerogative, his sole prerogative, to speak to the heart so as to make us foolish ones wise.
V. 61, p. 547

This is the very beginning of wisdom: to know the bitterness and mischief of sin, and to turn from it.
V. 61, p. 548

No one else can make a man wise, really, spiritually, internally, and eternally wise but God himself.
V. 61, p. 547

In nothing that God has done is there such a discovery of his wisdom as in the plan of redeeming love.
V. 8, p. 258

A wise man is a knowing man, although a knowing man is not always wise.
V. 61, p. 548

Were we always wise we would never murmur.
V. 45, p. 76

Were we to be endowed with infinite wisdom, we would rejoice in the very things which now distress us.
V. 45, p. 76

I think a man who says, "I was wrong," really in effect says, "I am a little wiser today than I was yesterday."
V. 45, p. 243

He who never admits that he has made a mistake, and claims that he has always been in the right, has evidently never made much growth in the knowledge of himself.
V. 45, p. 243

Where reason laboriously finds out wisdom, love discovers it at once.
V. 36, p. 51

I would rather be a fool and do what Christ tells me, than be the wisest man of the modern school, and despise the Word of the Lord.
V. 28, p. 216

O friends, be wise enough to be fools, and accept Jesus to be your wisdom.
V. 32, p. 502

Let us worship before the omnipotent Christ, to whom nothing is difficult, much less impossible.
V. 42, p. 99

WORLDLY INFLUENCE
∝

If you do not know how to stand fast against the world, you will find the world will stand fast against you.
V. 54, p. 251

Evil company is one of Satan's great nets in which he holds his birds until the time comes for their destruction.
V. 15, p. 285

How you deserve to perish who have not soul enough to call your soul your own, but cower down before the sneers of fools.
V. 15, p. 286

Men are so moved by the fear of contempt and poverty that they turn aside from the narrow path and no reasoning can convince them to follow it.
V. 15, p. 483

No earthly relationship can possibly help us if we are destitute of the spiritual life.
V. 25, p. 484

No pleasure of an hour can ever recompense for casting yourself under the anger of God forever and forever.
V. 61, p. 118

London's dens have in them many hapless profligates that are terrible warnings that men who seek their own pleasure put upon themselves a yoke of iron.
V. 18, p. 59

The world's pleasures grow more and more vapid and worthless, pleasures of idiots rather than men.
V. 12, p. 659

WORSHIP
∝

Offered without a sincere heart, every form of worship is a solemn sham and an impudent mockery of the majesty of heaven.
M. & E., p. 706

It is a necessity of your nature that you should have a god of some sort; and to prevent you from having a strange god, you must trust, cling to and love Jehovah, the one only living and true God.
V. 40, p. 457

A renewed soul yearns after that very intercourse which the formalist calls irreverent.
V. 10, p. 726

In intense devotion to the Lord you will find the rare jewel of satisfaction.
V. 27, p. 579

What God wants is the heart, the soul, the love, the trust, the confidence of rational, intelligent beings, not the going through of certain forms.
V. 61, p. 291

The forms (of worship) are useful enough when they teach us the truth of which they are the emblems but the mere form of outward worship is just nothing.
V. 61, p. 291

I love your simplicity (of worship), I admire it; but if you trust it, I believe your simplicity will as certainly ruin you as the gorgeousness that goes to the opposite extreme.
V. 61, p. 292

Let there be good music by all means, and noble words, for these are congruous to noble thoughts; but oh! let the thoughts be there; let the soul be there; let the flames of love burn on the altar of the heart.
V. 61, p. 293

The best worship comes from the Christian that is most tried.
V. 61, p. 298

Worship is the nearest approach to what it will be like in heaven, where day without night, they offer perpetual adoration unto him who sits upon the throne.
V. 46, p. 142

Keep all earthly treasures out of your heart, and let Christ be your treasure, and let him have your heart.
V. 50, p. 357

We need a holy fear of God, a sacred sense of God and a true delight in God.
V. 31, p. 436

Silence is as fit a garment for devotion as any that language can fashion.
V. 18, p. 134

We must worship him in spirit and in truth; not mechanically, as though we could have true fellowship with him without earnest and intense desire.
V. 42, p. 182

Many persons, in the public worship of God, sing simply because the time for singing has come.
V. 42, p. 99

He has better music than all your organs and drums can ever bring to him.
V. 38, p. 243

He may worship God who shouts until the earth rings again, and God may accept him; but he may worship God as truly who sits in silence before the Most High and says not a word.
V. 38, p. 29

We can sing high praises to ourselves when all is joyful; but we cannot sing praise to any save our God when circumstances are unfavorable and providence appears adverse.
V. 44, p. 99

God alone can give us songs in the night.
V. 44, p. 99

WRATH

Take heed, you that scorn the mercy-seat, lest it turn into a burning throne of wrath.
V. 28, p. 291

They that slight the warnings of God's grace shall feel the terrors of his wrath.
V. 16, p. 189

God grant that you may never know what it is to meet insulted love, rejected mercy, and tenderness turned to wrath.
V. 16, p. 189

The wrath of the Lamb is the most awful wrath beneath the sun.
V. 25, p. 442